Physical Ed

for T chers and Co ...
at Key S...

Sue Chedzoy

David Fulton Publishers

London

David Fulton Publishers Ltd
2 Barbon Close, London WC1N 3JX

First published in Great Britain by
David Fulton Publishers 1996

Note: The right of Sue Chedzoy to be identified as the author of this work has been asserted by her in accordance with the Copyright, Designs and Patents Act 1988.

British Library Cataloguing in Publication Data

A catalogue record for this book is available from the British Library

ISBN 1-85346-410-4

ERRATA

p.35, line 20	(DES, 1991c) should read (DES, 1992)
p.38, line 20	(see DES, 1991c) should read (see DES/WO, 1991b) which is not The Teaching and Learning of Physical Education, as inserted in the text, but the document Proposals of the Secretary of State for Education and Science and the Secretary of State for Wales.
p.45, line 8	(DES/WO, 1991b, p.9) should read (DES/WO, 1991a, p.9)
line 20	(DES/WO, 1991, p.9) should read (DES/WO, 1991a, p.9)
p.46, line 22	(DES/WO, 1991b) should read (DES/WO, 1991a, p.10)
p.89, line 19	DES survey (1991b) should read DES survey (1991c)

Typeset by Textype Typesetters, Cambridge
Printed in Great Britain by BPC Books and Journals Ltd, Exeter.

Contents

Preface

This book has been written to enable all those with responsibility for the teaching and managing of Physical Education to implement the National Curriculum for Physical Education at Key Stages 1 and 2.

Students on curriculum courses and those considering a curriculum leadership role in Physical Education will find the book a useful addition to the literature. For those teachers who are already working in schools the text is designed to focus on resources and approaches to achieve quality through balanced programmes of Physical Education in infant, junior, primary and middle schools.

Sue Chedzoy
Exeter, June 1996

Acknowledgements

I wish to thank Anita Davidson for her invaluable help with typing the manuscript. I also thank Nigel Weaver for the photographs and Central First School, Exeter, Central Middle School, Exeter and St Sidwells Combined School, Exeter for photographs of the children in action.

Extracts from *Physical Education in the National Curriculum Non-Statutory Guidance for Teachers* (1992) are reproduced with permission from the Curriculum and Assessment Authority for Wales, Cardiff.

CHAPTER 1

Physical Education in the National Curriculum – General Requirements

The National Curriculum for Physical Education (DFE, 1995a) for all year groups in Key Stages 1 and 2 became a legal requirement on 1 August 1995, by means of an Order made by the Secretaries of State for Education and for Wales. The Swimming Programme of Study for pupils in Years 5 and 6 comes into effect on 1 August 1996 and 1 August 1997 respectively.

Schools have been afforded a five year period of stability with the Schools Council Assessment Authority (SCAA) monitoring the implementation of the National Curriculum in schools.

In the new Order the General Requirements for Physical Education at Key Stages 1–4 are summarised:

> Physical Education should involve pupils in the continuous process of planning, performing and evaluating. The greatest emphasis should be placed on the actual performance aspect of the subject.
>
> (DFE, 1995a)

No one would deny that Physical Education is about doing and performing since in July 1990 the Physical Education Working Group appointed by the Secretary of State recommended:

> The attainment target for Physical Education should encompass the planning and the evaluating of activities, but the main emphasis should be on the participation, reflecting the active nature of the subject.
>
> (DES/WO, 1991a, p.1)

However it is vital that all those concerned with planning, teaching and assessing Physical Education at Key Stages 1 and 2 value children's contributions to the planning and evaluation of their own and others' work and do not simply pay attention to the performance aspect of the subject. For too long children and teachers have mainly judged success or failure in Physical Education in terms of performance. This poses no problem for the naturally athletic child or for children who have developed their skills and confidence through a range of activities, either during free play with friends or parents, or through organised sessions at clubs. However for many children Physical Education lessons have failed to instil positive feelings of self worth and achievement. When judged solely in terms of performance compared with that of fellow pupils, some children have left school feeling that they were 'no good' at Physical Education. Strictly speaking, it is not possible to be good or bad at Physical Education. Physical Education is a process of learning to enable young people develop physical competence, knowledge, skills and understanding through a balanced programme of activities which focuses on the child at his or her stage of development. It is through this process that children have an entitlement to learn to manage their bodies in a variety of situations, to acquire new skills and develop an understanding of what they are doing. It well may be that those failing children did not have the opportunity to be guided through a programme of differentiated tasks and a range of activities which stimulated their interest and helped them to feel confident and competent participants.

We shall have failed our young people if we do not fully involve them in this process of learning, giving them the best chance to discover pleasure in being active. If during this process children are given some responsibility and are actively involved in the planning, eg composing their own dances or creating simple games, they may gain a better understanding of the activities and also in assessment be given credit for contributing to the planning of their own work or that of others in a group.

Children's appreciation of good quality work may be enhanced by their experiences of evaluating their own work and that of others. For example children should be encouraged to look at gymnastic sequences to be able to identify the actions that have been included and comment on any changes of shape, speed or direction which are relevant to the task. Although particular children might not necessarily be able to perform to the same high standard themselves, they may be able to appreciate fine quality work, make relevant and critical comments and demonstrate a level of understanding and knowledge of the activity which should be recognised by a teacher assessing their contribution to the process.

The latest National Curriculum Order (DFE, 1995a) has omitted many explicit references to planning and evaluating in the Programmes of Study. However teachers and students will be well advised to emphasise these aspects, alongside the performance in planning and delivering the curriculum. This emphasis will have implications for the teaching styles employed, encouraging children to take responsibility for their own learning. The three strands – planning, performing, evaluating – relate quite naturally to approaches taken in other areas of the primary curriculum, ie Art and Music, where children are given responsibility for creating, performing and appreciating their own work and the work of others.

General Requirements for Physical Education

This section follows the 'General Requirements for Physical Education' as set out in *Physical Education in the National Curriculum* (DFE, 1995a). These apply to the teaching of Physical Education across all Key Stages and each aspect will be considered in relation to the teaching of Physical Education in Key Stages 1 and 2. Teachers and students will need to address these issues when teaching Physical Education in primary schools.

1. To promote physical activity and healthy life styles, pupils should be taught:

(a) *to be physically active*

Research has shown that children as young as 10 years old are not experiencing the volume of physical activity that is believed to promote health-related outcomes (Armstrong and Bray, 1991; Sleap and Warburton, 1992).

The Allied Dunbar National Fitness Survey (1992) of adults' fitness revealed low levels of physical activity, aerobic fitness and muscular strength in older people. The survey indicated that those citizens who had engaged in physical activity during childhood were more likely to participate in health-related physical activity as adults.

It is most important that children are taught how to be physically active from an early age. They should be encouraged to experience a variety of physical activities, so that they are able to discover activities that they enjoy and in which they gain some success. Young children need safe free play areas. They also need to know where to go to find organised activities and what is expected of them when they attend such activities in the community. Sometimes children worry about what they should wear, where they should store their clothes when at the leisure centre or whether they will be good enough to take part in the activities. Children with parents or relatives who take them to clubs, leisure centres

4

or on activity holidays have an advantage over others who might have more limited resources. Teachers can help young children to feel more comfortable in such situations by talking them over in class or by arranging a trip to the local sports centre or swimming pool as a class activity.

In class children can be encouraged to tell their peers about the physical activities that they enjoy in their leisure time, perhaps prompting others to try something different. By sharing ideas with each other pupils and their teachers may find opportunities which might not otherwise have been identified. For example they might:

- share transport, taking friends along to join in activities in the evening, at weekends or during the holidays;
- share equipment, eg skateboards, frisbees or music tapes for dancing;
- organise fun runs, health weeks, clubs for skipping, judo, swimming, dancing and skating.

Such activities, whether organised in school or in the community, should be made accessible to all, not just to those who feel competent and confident to take part.

Children of all abilities should be taught and encouraged to be active. Too often activity clubs have only been open to the more able performers who are talented enough to be in the 'team'. Of course there should be chances for more able performers to enjoy excelling in activities. However, all concerned with the provision of physical activities for young children need to be aware that attitudes towards physical activity are often formed in childhood and taken into adult life. It is unacceptable that young children should ever feel that they are not good enough to take part. It is the responsibility of parents, teachers and professionals in the community to offer children opportunities to succeed and become skilful, to have some fun and to feel comfortable in the environment so that when they have choices they opt for active healthy lifestyles.

Children need to be exposed to a range of physical activities in school to develop a repertoire of motor skills which will enable them to take part happily in physical activity for pleasure. If girls in the junior school are only offered a diet of netball for their games experience, it will be the tall girls and the agile ones who stand the best chances of being successful. When teaching in the secondary phase I was always saddened to hear children announce during their first term, 'I'm no good at PE Miss!' It often transpired that what they meant was, 'I'm no good at netball Miss' because that was all they had experienced in Physical Education. Similarly not all boys enjoy football and if this is their sole experience of games in the primary school, then they are likely to develop negative

COMMENT ON GIRLS - NETBALL'.

feelings towards Physical Education from an early age.

The National Curriculum for Physical Education has now secured for our children an entitlement to a well-delivered, broad and balanced programme which should offer all children a chance to develop skills and positive attitudes to various forms of physical activity. All those concerned with teaching Physical Education should be sensitive to children's needs and endeavour to make those early experiences enjoyable.

Children need to understand some very simple concepts about the effects of exercise on the body. The evidence that physical activity has health-giving benefits is unequivocal (Powell et al., 1987) and the facts about exercise can be taught in the classroom, perhaps through Science and Health Education, as well as in the Physical Education lessons. Resources are available to support this aspect of the curriculum (Happy Heart Project, Health Education Authority 1990; My Body Project, Health Education Authority 1991; British Heart Foundation, 1995). The more confident and skilful children become, the more likely will they be to choose to be active throughout their lives.

(b) *to adopt the best possible posture and the appropriate use of the body*

In 1933 the Board of Education issued the Syllabus of Physical Training for Schools (Board of Education, 1933). It was written to support elementary school teachers in the delivery of Physical Education. It is of interest to note that inspectors visiting schools at that time would judge the effectiveness of the class teacher by the posture of the children in their classes. It was assumed that if children stood, sat and presented themselves in an upright and smart manner then the teacher was doing a good job. Ever since then, posture has rarely been mentioned in guidance from central government in relation to Physical Education. However, as the focus of Physical Education is to do with the development and management of the body, then it would seem sensible that it should be through this area of the curriculum that children are made aware of the importance of good posture in their everyday lives. It is heartening to see this aspect of education featured in the general requirements.

Teachers should use every opportunity to encourage good posture, for example in teaching safe walking, sitting and standing positions and teaching young children good movement habits. Children from as early as the reception phase should be taught to adopt the appropriate posture when landing from jumping activities, they should be encouraged to bend their knees and give in the ankles on impact and use the arms for balance. The concept of squashy landings can be taught from an early age. The children should also be taught to vary the direction and speed of running to avoid collisions with others. Young children can learn to pace themselves and judge distances and respond appropriately in a variety of situations. These habits will help them to prepare for situations they will encounter through their lives at home and during play.

(c) *to engage in activities that develop cardiovascular health, flexibility, muscular strength and endurance*

Non-specialist primary teachers might wonder how to teach children to engage in activities that develop cardiovascular health, flexibility, muscular strength and endurance. They will be reassured to realise that a sound, well-balanced curriculum in which children experience all the requirements of the Programmes of Study at Key Stages 1 and 2 should achieve these ends. Cardiovascular health refers to the efficient functioning of the circulatory and respiratory systems, an aspect of fitness sometimes called stamina. Children can begin to understand that the fitness of their heart and lungs may be maintained and improved by regular aerobic exercise activities such as swimming, jogging, cycling, dancing, skipping and brisk walking. The running and chasing games that young children often enjoy and play spontaneously will contribute to the development of their cardiovascular health. Some excellent resources have been developed for teachers to help children to learn about the function and maintenance of the cardiovascular system, see British Heart Foundation, 1995; Happy Heart Project, Health Education Authority 1990; My Body Project, Health Education Authority 1991; Action for Heart Health, Harris and Elbourn 1990.

Gymnastic activities and dance are areas of the curriculum which can positively affect children's flexibility. Flexibility refers to mobility of the joints of the body, and children can be taught to understand the value of regular stretching exercises to maintain and enhance joint mobility. This is achievable through the Physical Education programme by children experiencing stretching and mobilising activities as part of their warm-up programme. Within gymnastics and dance lessons children should be given opportunities to develop a repertoire of movement which will help them to maintain and increase their flexibility.

Healthy children develop increased strength as they mature. Opportunities to run, jump, throw, balance, climb and swing will facilitate this development. Pre-adolescent children should not be involved in weightlifting because of possible damage to the growth zones of the skeleton. However children can have a great deal of fun and derive benefit from exercises such as safe sit-ups, push-ups and partner activities involving friendly contests of strength against each other. Teachers' resources are available to teach this aspect of the curriculum

(Bray, 1993; Sleap, 1995).

(d) *pupils should be taught the increasing need for personal hygiene in relation to physical activity*

Few primary schools are able to offer pupils shower facilities for use after physical activities. Schools offering a swimming programme have the opportunity to teach children basic habits of hygiene, such as visiting the toilet before swimming, using the footbath and showering before and after entering the pool.

Children need to be taught that when they exercise more vigorously their skin becomes hotter and they perspire more freely. They should be told about anti-perspirants that reduce the amount of sweat produced by the body and that deodorants destroy bacteria that cause body odour. Children should understand that once air gets to the sweat and bacteria begins to breed it starts to smell rather unpleasant and that the problem can be overcome by washing regularly with soap. They should also recognise the value of frequently changing clothes which have been worn for exercise.

2. To develop positive attitudes, pupils should be taught:

(a) *to observe the conventions of fair play, honest competition and good sporting behaviour as individual participants, team members and spectators*

Throughout their years in the Primary school children should be encouraged to develop a sense of social responsibility and a value for and sensitivity towards individual differences. Within the Physical Education programme there should be a balance between cooperative and competitive activities. Children should be encouraged to adopt good sporting behaviour and be offered opportunities to discuss the nature of appropriate behaviour, anti-social behaviour and the issue of cheating, and make judgements.

Children can be helped to distinguish good from bad behaviour and their views should be considered from an early age. Discussions about sporting behaviour may arise from incidents which children may have seen on television involving well-known sportsmen and women. Even though these personalities do not always present good role models for our young people, their behaviour can stimulate debate about standards and values in sport.

From an early age, even when working individually, children should be encouraged to develop appropriate codes of conduct. They should be encouraged to:

- persevere with tasks;
- be honest when keeping scores or measuring achievements;
- enable others around them to engage in tasks without any interference;
- to cooperate when working as a team and to accept the rules of the activity;
- observe safe practice at all times.

Children who are given responsibility for planning and preparation for participation from an early age are more able to accept rules and conventions of fair play than those who always have rules imposed upon them by the teacher. For example, children who have had opportunities to make up their own rules for games are likely to play to them and sort out any problems amongst themselves because they have some ownership of the structure and see the sense of the rules. Similarly children who are given responsibility to compose their own dances and gymnastic sequences in pairs and groups need to cooperate and respect each others' views in order to reach a consensus and create the finished piece of work.

At Key Stage 1 and throughout Key Stage 2 the foundations should be laid to enable children to be informed spectators. They should be encouraged to develop a vocabulary with which to describe movement, demonstrating an understanding of what they observe. This will only happen if teachers allow plenty of time for children to watch a range of activities either in class, through the use of television and video, or perhaps giving children a chance to see professionals demonstrating their skills and sharing their expertise. This might be achieved through viewing the performance of a professional dance company and talking to the artists about the work.

(b) *how to cope with success and limitations in performance*

Within the Physical Education programme and during extracurricular activities children can be taught to recognise successes in their own endeavours and learn how to deal with them without intimidating others. Children should be encouraged to take a pride in good performance and recognise and value their own and others' achievements.

Opportunities will arise which will require children to persevere with difficult tasks and be sensitive to difficulties encountered by others. Children should be taught how to cooperate, share expertise in group situations and be tolerant and patient with each other.

(c) *to try hard to consolidate their performance*

Within all Programmes of Study children should be encouraged to realise that if they try hard and concentrate on learning new skills it will enable them to enjoy a variety of activities at school, at home and in the community, which will enhance their lifestyles and positively affect their health.

(d) *to be mindful of others and the environment*

All physical activities involve some interaction between individuals and groups and from an early age children should be taught to consider others in planning, performing and evaluating their activities.

Children should learn to care for the equipment that they use and take a pride in handling it in the proper manner, and returning it with due consideration for others to use afterwards.

Children should be aware of the space in which they are working in Physical Education and be alert to any restrictions or limitations in that working environment. The Outdoor and Adventurous Activities Programme of Study at Key Stage 2 presents ideal opportunities to heighten children's awareness and respect for their environment.

3. To ensure safe practice, pupils should be taught:

(a) *to respond readily to instructions*

It is important that children learn to listen to instructions and in Physical Education this is not always easy as lessons take place in large spaces which may not be acoustically perfect. A whole school approach can be helpful here, with staff agreeing on the strategies which will best suit the environment. For example, in Gymnastics Activities lessons the level of noise should be such that, if the teacher wishes to talk to the class while they are on apparatus, it should be necessary only to raise the voice for the children to respond immediately. Children should be encouraged to be alert and to listen carefully to instructions in the realisation that prompt responses may prevent accidents.

The use of a whistle should not be necessary in Gymnastics and Dance lessons. However, in teaching Games outside on the field or playground, or Swimming at the poolside, the use of a whistle can be helpful in alerting children to the next activity. Children should be taught to listen carefully to instructions especially in regard to the safety of themselves and others – for example, in Athletics Activities they should listen to the advice given on safety in throwing, keeping within boundaries, and landings in jumping activities. At all times children should be encouraged to understand the necessity for listening carefully in Physical Education. They must realise that injuries may be caused if they are careless and that their safety and that of others depends on them being good listeners.

(b) *to recognise and follow relevant rules, laws, codes, etiquette and safety procedures for different activities or events, in practice and in competition*

Safety must be paramount in the minds of all involved in the Physical Education programme so that children acquire a respect for safe practice in relation to all their activities. The foundation for safe practice should be laid from the moment children arrive in school and a coordinated approach by staff should ensure that children take progressively more responsibility for their own code of conduct. It is the teacher's responsibility to make the codes of behaviour quite clear to children as they work in different environments. This will require a whole school approach with all staff agreeing the practice with regard to safety in the hall, playground and field and when travelling to off-site facilities. All Programmes of Study need to be considered and safety procedures agreed.

Children need to be taught that activities are performed within a framework of rules and laws which are constructed to provide a fair and safe environment. They need to understand the reasons for adherence to rules and the importance of keeping to them.

In the Programme of Study for Games at Key Stage 2 small-sided games are recommended. If children have been making up their own simple games and rules individually and in pairs at Key Stage 1 and in the early stages of Key Stage 2, the transition to playing small-sided 3 v 3, 4 v 4, and 5 v 5 games together is made easier for teachers to organise. Many teachers feel rather daunted at the thought of having several small-sided games being played simultaneously, as they feel children might be unable to cope with supervising their own play without teacher intervention. However, if through the primary years children have been gradually introduced to this approach, they will be used to resolving problems and playing cooperatively within their own rules. This releases the teacher from a refereeing role, providing time to move around the groups to facilitate learning and the application of skills and tactics. This approach also helps children to come to terms with the need for rules and laws and the importance of keeping to them in their play.

The etiquette associated with particular activities can be discussed informally in the classroom. It is quite common for children of primary school age to be involved in ballet, football, judo, horse riding, sailing and a host of other activities in the community. Sports and activities bring with them particular etiquettes which might be of interest when discussed and shared with all children in the class. It is certainly helpful for children to have a knowledge of the codes of behaviour expected of them if they have the opportunity to participate.

Through experiencing competition between classes, houses and inter-school matches children can develop and practice socially acceptable behaviour when entertaining other teams, and learn to be generous to others whatever the result of the contest.

(c) *about the safety risks of wearing inappropriate clothing, footwear and jewellery, and why particular clothing, footwear and protection are worn for different activities*

All schools should have a policy relating to the clothing that should be worn for Physical Education lessons throughout the school. This should be agreed and adhered to by all staff so that children and parents are aware of the standards that are expected of them as they move through the school. The kit should be chosen for comfort, practical use and with safety in mind. For example, large baggy T-shirts which may be currently fashionable are not suitable for Gymnastics Activities. Children may get them caught up on apparatus and they are also impractical when children are upside down. If T-shirts are worn they should be tucked in for safety.

Some schools adopt a different set of kit for indoor and outdoor activities. It is most important that children are warm enough when working outside as negative attitudes may develop if children associate Physical Education with feeling cold and uncomfortable. Tracksuits and jogging bottoms are relatively inexpensive, and allowing children to wear them and to shed a layer after the warm-up may go a long way to encourage enjoyable participation.

Consideration must be given to requirements relating to the cultural differences of children in the school. Clothing worn for activities needs to be in accord with religious teachings and suitable clothes can be agreed between parents and teachers.

Footwear is a major consideration in Physical Education. Barefoot work is recommended for indoor work in Gymnastics Activities and Dance as long as the floor is clean and splinter free; but if footwear needs to be worn, light gymnastic shoes or plimsoles, or dance shoes are suitable. Heavy training shoes should never be worn for these activities as it is difficult for children to grip whilst wearing them on apparatus or to develop resilience and light foot work. Children should understand the reasons for their unsuitability and be encouraged to be suitably equipped for Dance and Gymnastics Activities.

If children understand the reasons for changing into appropriate clothing for different activities they are more likely to adhere to the conventions required by the school. It has to be said that pupils' feelings and views have not always been considered in the selection of clothing for Physical Education and schools need to think about what will best suit all pupils. Some children from an early age feel self-conscious when asked to take part in Physical Education lessons stripped to their underwear – common practice in some infant and first schools. Although it saves time spent in changing, schools need to consider such a policy carefully in the light of discussions. Similarly, consideration should be given to the issue of girls wearing leotards as large and mature girls do not always feel happy performing Athletics, Dance or Gymnastics Activities wearing leotards and might feel less inhibited wearing shorts or leggings and tops.

Long hair should always be tied back for any aspect of Physical Education, and for Gymnastics Activities a soft tie rather than a hard bobble will be more comfortable, especially when children are attempting inversion activities such as headstands.

All jewellery should be removed for any physical activities and children should be told the reason for this as it has implications for the safety of themselves and others. It is quite common for boys and girls to have their ears pierced and they should be discouraged from wearing their earrings to school on days timetabled for Physical Education. If children are unable to remove their jewellery for religious reasons, if possible it should be taped and parents need to be aware of implications with regard to safety.

(d) *how to lift and carry, place and use equipment safely*

Millions of working days are missed each year through back pain. Many of these problems might be avoided if all had been taught to lift and carry correctly from an early age. Teachers should use every opportunity to help children to understand that correct lifting and carrying skills are important. Although children rarely suffer from back pain it will prepare the foundations for future good practice. It is especially within Gymnastics Activities lessons that children should be given opportunities to lift, carry and place apparatus correctly . Children should be encouraged to keep a straight back when lifting, pushing and pulling, to know that they should get down to the level of the load by bending hips and knees and that they should stand close to the object with feet apart and facing the direction of the move. Children – even as early as the reception phase – need to cooperate and concentrate when moving a load as a group and when lifting and carrying heavy items. It is worthwhile spending time with children, helping them to master correct techniques, as this will develop life skills which in future might positively affect their health. Teachers should not be tempted to deny children these opportunities by employing older children or the caretaker to set out the gymnastics apparatus.

The use of apparatus should be discussed by staff and some principles agreed for a whole school approach. This will make it easier for children to progress through the school safely using more complex apparatus.

(e) *to warm-up for and recover from exercise*

Children need to understand why warming-up is important. They need to understand that the heart is a muscle and like any other muscle it needs to have exercise to keep it strong. They also need to know that the heart acts as a pump to circulate the blood, increasing the provision of oxygen to muscles during exercise. It should be explained that before any more vigorous exercise the heart rate should be gradually increased. Resting heart rates for children are approximately 80 beats per minute (slightly higher than for adults) and during vigorous exercise children's heart rates may be raised to over 200 beats per minute.

The warm-up needs to be appropriate for the activity. It should prepare the body both physically and mentally for the activity to follow. The required physiological responses can be attained by asking children to simply run around the field or the hall for a few minutes at the start of the lesson. However, if the warm-up activity not only raises the pulse rate but also sets the scene for further activities it will probably be more enjoyable and worthwhile for all concerned – for example, in Dance lessons travelling about the space to the lively rhythm of music, refining stepping, turning and jumping patterns; in Games and Athletics Activities playing running and tag games; and in Gymnastics Activities travelling in a variety of ways about the space following different pathways alone or with others.

After the pulse raising activities and once the body becomes warmer then the muscles may be gently stretched and the joints mobilised. Thinking of the muscles as elastic bands that need to be gently stretched can help children to understand this concept.

Even during the primary phase children can perform simple warming-up and cooling-down activities independently if they have been guided through a variety of ideas during their Physical Education lessons. There are resources of imaginative ideas for warming-up and cooling-down activities which are available for teachers to use across all Programmes of Study (Bray, 1993; Harris and Elbourn, 1990).

These General Requirements must be considered by all staff involved in planning and teaching the Physical Education curriculum at Key Stages 1 and 2 .

In addition, the following introductory paragraphs at each Key Stage have been written into the revised Order to reflect the scope, character

14

and objectives of Physical Education. These are statutory requirements and underpin the whole Physical Education curriculum.

Key Stage 1 Programme of Study

In each year of the Key Stage, pupils should be taught three areas of activity: Games, Gymnastics and Dance, using indoor and outdoor environments where appropriate. In addition, schools may choose to teach Swimming in Key Stage 1 using the Programme of Study set out in Key Stage 2.

Throughout the Key Stage, pupils should be taught:

- about the changes that occur to their bodies as they exercise
- to recognise the short-term effects of exercise on the body. (p.3)

Key Stage 2 Programme of Study

Pupils should be taught six areas of activity. During each year of the Key Stage pupils should be taught Games, Gymnastics Activities and Dance. At points during the Key Stage pupils should be taught Athletics Activities, Outdoor and Adventurous Activities and Swimming unless they have already completed the Programme of Study for Swimming during Key Stage 1. If aspects of the Swimming programme have been taught during Key Stage 1, pupils should be taught the Key Stage 2 Swimming programme starting at the appropriate point.

Throughout the Key Stage, pupils should be taught:

- how to sustain energetic activity over appropriate periods of time in a range of physical activities
- the short-term effects of exercise on the body. (p.4)

These are challenges which face all those concerned with teaching Physical Education in primary schools. In the following chapters issues are raised and explored which will help teachers to manage and deliver high quality programmes of Physical Education.

CHAPTER 2

The Role and Responsibilities of the Curriculum Coordinator for Physical Education

Traditionally, primary teachers in most schools have taught a single class across the full range of the primary curriculum. To meet the requirements of the National Curriculum, and the need for more systematic coverage of all subjects in all classes, many schools now find it helpful to identify coordinators with strengths in particular subjects who can assist and help train other staff.

(DFE, 1995, *Circular 14/93*)

The Primary Schools Survey (DES, 1978) raised the status and importance of the role of curriculum coordinators in Primary schools. The survey revealed evidence to show that when teachers were able to exercise influence through the planning and supervision of a programme of work, standards of achievement were raised. However, in spite of HMI extolling the virtues of teachers taking responsibility for coordinating areas of the curriculum, the survey revealed that in reality many teachers had little influence on the quality of work in other classrooms:

8.45. It is disappointing to find that the great majority of teachers with posts of responsibility have little influence at present on the work of other teachers. Consideration needs to be given to improving their standing which is the product of the ways in which the teachers with special posts regard themselves and also of the attitudes that other teachers have towards them.

8.46. It is important that teachers with special responsibility for, say mathematics should, in consultation with the head, other members of staff and teachers in neighbouring schools, draw up the scheme of work to be implemented in the school; give guidance and support to other members of staff; assist in mathematics to other classes when necessary; and be responsible for the procurement, within the funds made available, of the necessary resources for the teaching of the subject. They should develop acceptable means of assessing the effectiveness of the guidance and resources they provide, and this may involve visiting other classes in the school to see the work in progress. (p.119)

With regard to Physical Education it is surprising to note in the 1978 survey that in schools with less than a three form entry:

4.4 Posts with special responsibility for games were more common than posts for mathematics. (p.37)

The House of Commons Select Committee (1986) also made a persuasive case for coordinators and suggested ways forward to develop curriculum management and school development.

Holly and Southworth (1989) summarised the findings of researchers who studied curriculum coordination during the 1980s:

• School based development is complex and it involves three factors:

 - teachers working in partnership
 - exchange of expertise
 - compatible relationships in respect of authority, classroom autonomy and curriculum activity.

• Job descriptions not only describe tasks expected of individuals; they also reflect messages about harmony and authority in the school.
• Personal qualities of the coordinator and the ability to gain respect of their colleagues have a profound effect on the authority of the coordinator.
• Lack of time to implement the role was a major problem.
• Many coordinators found it difficult to direct colleagues and often lacked the confidence to act as a critical friend.
• Limited INSET provision for coordinators restricted their opportunities to develop interpersonal skills.
• The extent to which headteachers enabled coordinators to function effectively varied considerably. Coordinators expressed a need for more generous allowance of time and money and more opportunity for personal development and authority.
• Cross curricular issues were underdeveloped because the curriculum focus was mainly subject based.

They identified the main lessons learned from the 1980s to improve the effectiveness of coordinators in the future. Coordinators will need to develop skills in:

- interpreting the curriculum, managing change and evaluating outcomes
- relating to colleagues
- identifying potential partners to provide external support
- understanding school cultures and recognising factors which encourage collaboration and development.

Headteachers need to support coordinators by:

- offering time for coordinators to observe and work with colleagues.

They also need to provide opportunities for coordinators to:

- lead meetings and workshops
- liaise with governors and parents
- purchase resources.

It was recognised that someone on the management team should have an overview of the work of coordinators and coordinate their work throughout the school.

Day et al. (1993) saw the role of the curriculum coordinator as being central to the development of the school in four ways. In their view coordinators should contribute to:

- The school development plan with coordinators bringing knowledge of the teaching and learning of their subject within the school.
- The school culture and the relationships within it, coordinators should play a significant role in shaping its development.
- Educative leadership, defined as 'helping professional educators work with others to shape their purposes and the meanings that they use to make sense of, and justify their involvement in and the contribution to education'. The authors advise that 'Being an "educative" leader means recognising, for example that your colleagues learn naturally, though not all in the same ways or at the same rate. Like you, they will be at different stages of their career development. It is important to recognise, for example, that some may be less enthusiastic and have less energy than you for perfectly acceptable reasons. Your "intervention" in their learning worlds must relate to their learning contexts.' (p.6)
- A vision for future developments by being reflective practicioners.

The authors offered coordinators a range of activities and strategies for leading change through staff development, developing assertiveness skills and ways forward in creating a community of enquiry. Any person undertaking a coordinator role will find the text both thought-provoking and informative.

Day, Whitaker and Johnson (1990) focused attention on the need for a collaborative approach to management for effective leadership.

> The kind of management structure more likely to be successful in meeting the challenges of the future is one that makes optimum use of the human resources at its disposal. This will not only require the skilful combining of individual strengths and abilities but a capacity to build group and partnership skills within the working team. (p.35)

They highlighted the need for schools to accommodate the needs of the whole staff and through team effort create opportunities for school development. These findings and issues will be considered in relation to coordinating Physical Education.

Coordinating Physical Education at Key Stages 1 and 2

Where do I begin?

   Secure a clearly defined job description and negotiate a budget and a time to implement the role

   Develop and refine your own good practice

   Review the provision of:
   - resources
   - documentation
   - facilities
   - time allocation for physical education

Where do I go from here?

   Talk to staff informally about teaching and learning in Physical Education
   - recognise strengths
   - clarify any barriers to development

   Consider the place of Physical Education in the School Development Plan

   In consultation with staff begin to formulate strategies for short, medium and long term planning

---

Figure 2.1 Curriculum coordination in Physical Education

The most recent review of good practice (DES/WO, 1991c) revealed that effective curriculum coordinators have a noticeable influence on the quality of work in Physical Education throughout the school. It also indicated that those who had the strongest influence on the quality of work were mostly experienced teachers. However, because of the active nature of the subject and the low status afforded to it in some schools (Evans, 1993) it seems that the responsibility for coordinating Physical Education is often given to young and rather inexperienced teachers who demonstrate more enthusiasm for the subject than knowledge. It would seem helpful therefore to offer some strategies to assist both experienced and inexperienced coordinators to tackle the role. Harrison and Theaker (1989) offered useful advice for curriculum coordinators and suggested that they negotiate with the headteacher:

- a specific aspect to be concentrated upon
- a target date for completion of specified, agreed objectives
- an allocation of school session time, if appropriate
- a financial allocation for resources, if appropriate/possible
- attendance at appropriate in-service courses
- a clearly understood intended outcome from the activity.

This process will allow you and the headteacher to formulate a coherent, realistic and achievable action plan. (p.8)

Job Descriptions

Advertisements for postholders will often give an indication of the value afforded to the subject and the way in which it is taught in the school. Most advertisements outline the requirements quite clearly. However it would be important to think carefully before replying to one simply requiring, for example, 'a person to coordinate either girls/boys games'. Such advertisements do exist and tend to indicate the way the area of activity is taught in the school, which is not always in line with National Curriculum requirements. Alternatively such an advertisement could reflect shared responsibility for aspects of Physical Education which, for a newly qualified teacher, might be more appealing than managing the whole Physical Education curriculum. If in doubt about the nature of the post do contact the school to discuss the role prior to application.

What is certain is that clearly defined job descriptions are very useful for teachers who are about to assume responsibility for a curriculum area. Once appointed, a written description of the role and responsibilities needs to be established. Make sure that you know what powers are afforded to you and that you are aware of the boundaries in which you are expected to operate. However, as Harrison and Cross (1994) cautioned, job descriptions which are too highly prescriptive leave little scope for individual enterprise and initiative. Schools also need to recognise the prior experience of the coordinator, and job specifications should reflect different expectations of a newly appointed coordinator to one who has spent a number of years in post.

Whatever the experience of the candidate, an enabling and supportive structure within the school in which managerial responsibility is made explicit is essential.

Time

The extra demands of a curriculum coordinator's role can to some degree be offset if you are able to secure some non-teaching time in which to fulfil your subject responsibilities. OFSTED (1995a) reported that coordinators need more non-teaching time to provide support for other colleagues. This might require you to negotiate with the headteacher quite early in the appointment and this will be made easier if, prior to the meeting, you have considered ways in which you might use that time. Certain aspects of the role can only be tackled when the school is in session – for example, reflecting on and assessing the teaching and learning in Physical Education throughout the school, observing lessons and offering teaching support to colleagues.

As Harrison and Theaker (1989) pointed out, 'The effective management of time will play a key part in determining the quality of your success as a curriculum leader and it is necessary to keep this under constant review'. They offered good advice to teachers who are unable to secure non-contact time – suggesting that setting clear targets and giving those a high priority will be a positive way forward, especially if realistic time-scales are established. 'There is only a certain amount of time available and it may mean a prioritising of priorities' (p.8).

In small schools where it might be difficult to secure non-contact time some shared teaching or investment in supply cover can help coordinators to facilitate their role.

Most teachers recognise that there never seems enough time to fulfil all aspects of teaching in a Primary school and they might consider some strategies for more effective time management, for example:

- being realistic in setting goals;
- keeping a diary, logging on a daily or weekly basis how time is spent;
- noting priorities and allocating time to address those issues;
- establishing project completion dates for specified, agreed objectives;

- learning to decline invitations to take on additional tasks or responsibilities;
- allocating special time for personal development.

Negotiate a budget

The school development plan will give an indication of the amount of money allocated to Physical Education both in the short and long term. An annual allowance of approximately £500 will ensure that items of small equipment, eg bats, balls, shuttlecocks, beachballs, swimming floats may be replaced and new items bought. It is important to think of these items as consumables, as inevitably some get lost or damaged through use. However if larger pieces of equipment need to be purchased it might be necessary to negotiate with the headteacher and the governors for a 'one off' payment, in which instance it might be that your bid is in competition with other subject areas. In making the case identify:

- How often the equipment will be used.
- Who will use it – the whole school? infants? juniors? Will there be any joint school and community use? Will the equipment be shared with other schools?
- When will it be used? Will this be during curriculum time or during extracurricular activities?

Be prepared to explain:

- The educational value of the equipment for the pupils.
- How the equipment might make organisation or management easier for staff and pupils.

As coordinator you might consider seeking funding from other sources, for example the Parent Teacher Association, or perhaps, if facilities will be shared with the community, National Lottery funds. Some schools do organise special events – such as sponsored skipping, swimming or *It's a Knockout*-type activities to raise money for specific items of equipment or to improve facilities.

Manufacturers will send a free price-list and brochures of equipment on request. You might need to check prices and also find out whether there is a local consortium from which you could purchase equipment at more competitive rates. Sometimes it is difficult to judge the quality of products by just looking at a picture in a brochure. If in any doubt about what to buy, make arrangements to visit other schools, consult with colleagues or attend the exhibition of physical education equipment which is displayed at the Annual Conference of the Physical Education

Association of the United Kingdom (PEA UK). A list of firms supplying equipment and the address of the PEA UK will be found in Chapter 5.

Be a good role model and lead by example

As coordinator for Physical Education you need to keep up to date with current ideas and issues in the subject. Carney (1994) revealed the latest figures in relation to time devoted to Physical Education in initial teacher training and it seems possible that even though you might have responsibility and enthusiasm for this area of the curriculum your initial teacher training course might have been 30 hours or less. OFSTED (1995a) are aware that some teachers who coordinate Physical Education have limited expertise in the subject.

If you are newly appointed to a school do take the time to develop your own good practice with your own class before you attempt to influence the work of others. There are several sources which you might find useful in keeping you up to date with developments. The lead body for Physical Education is the PEA UK and it publishes the *British Journal of Physical Education* and the *Primary Focus* which includes articles on research, teaching and learning in Physical Education, reviews of books and resources, and details of courses for teachers both in the United Kingdom and abroad. The British Association of Advisers and Lecturers in Physical Education (BAALPE), the National Dance Teachers Association, the Outdoor Education Association also offer support for teachers in the form of publications, courses and resources.

The Local Education Authority (LEA) reorganisation in the early 1990s saw a reduction of numbers of LEA advisers. However in 1996 it is heartening to notice the increased number of advertisements in the professional press for more subject specialist advisers to support the teaching and learning of Physical Education in schools. If you identify an area in your expertise in which you feel you need more support, the local Adviser or Inspector will be able to help you with curriculum support and provide details of relevant courses or conferences. Some authorities provide advisory teachers or curriculum support teachers who are able to visit your school and work alongside you in planning and teaching an aspect of the curriculum in which you need some help.

Develop your own good practice

In the areas in which you do feel confident, try to develop your own skills. Leading by example can be a powerful way to help others understand good practice. Expect high standards of achievement from your own class. Always ensure that you and the children are appropriately dressed for Physical Education lessons. However do resist the temptation to wear your tracksuit around the school all day.

Develop and establish safe and good practice when teaching in the hall, on the field or at the swimming pool. The fact that Physical Education is taught in large open spaces can be a bonus as other teachers often see what is going on in ways which would not always be possible if you were working in a closed classroom. In this way you might just influence the work of others. Use a variety of strategies to manage and organise the children and create every opportunity to enable them to plan and evaluate their work as well as encouraging them to perform to the best of their ability. You might find that teachers will comment informally about what they see and ask you questions about Physical Education. Certainly, if you are able to demonstrate good practice it will go a long way towards winning their confidence in you as a coordinator.

You might consider other ways in which your good practice could be shared informally with others, for example:

- arranging opportunities for children to give dance or gymnastics performances for whole school assemblies,
- videoing children's work to use as a starting point for discussion;
- displaying photographs, in the hall or corridors, showing children involved in various aspects of Physical Education, eg a trip to a local beach or woodland, swimming, demonstrating athletics events;
- mounting written work in which children have described their experiences in Physical Education – how it felt to cooperate in a group in some problem-solving activities, what stimulated a dance idea;
- displaying art work depicting children in action;
- providing opportunities for children to tell others about their involvement in aspects of physical activity, eg a competition against another school, attendance at a club activity.

Rationale

You need to have a well reasoned rationale for inclusion of the subject in the curriculum and be able to articulate that to colleagues. One of the most useful documents to refer to is the Proposals of the Secretary of State for Education and Science and the Secretary of State for Wales (DES/WO, 1991b). In this document there are comprehensive chapters addressing special educational needs, assessment, cross-curricular matters, and partners in provision relating to Physical Education.

Familarise yourself with the National Curriculum document for

Physical Education (DFE, 1995a) and if necessary be prepared to interpret the requirements within it for colleagues. The reduction in content from earlier documents (DES/WO, 1991a; DES, 1992) does not necessarily mean that teachers will find the most recent document easy to put into practice. If you have sound subject knowledge it will give you confidence to discuss matters with colleagues. Curriculum expertise was identified by Alexander (1992) as a factor of success in curriculum coordination.

It is important that you help to promote a well balanced curriculum in the school and as coordinator do not give the impression that some areas of the programme are more valuable than others. A love of football, a passion for dance, a personal interest in athletics, swimming or outdoor activities can be a bonus if children are offered the benefit of a particular expertise or enthusiasm as long as it is not detrimental to the development of other areas of the curriculum.

Review the provision of resources

As a coordinator you will be involved in managing both human and physical resources. If you are an inexperienced curriculum coordinator you might find that the least threatening starting point for implementing the role is with a review of resources and facilities. It is easier to deal with things than people.

- Make an audit of equipment and apparatus on and off site.
- Identify any resources which need replacing, discarding, updating, mending or improving.
- Catalogue the supply and circulate it to all staff.

Unless the list has been regularly updated it is possible that some staff will be unaware of the full range of available resources. Seek out any hidden supplies which may have found their way into individual teacher's classrooms and as a consequence have not been available for general use. Invite colleagues to a meeting to offer suggestions and to provide examples of any resources that they have used and feel might benefit the school as a whole. This will create an opportunity to discuss provision together and to identify priorities for future purchases.

Try to make the subject's presence felt around the school and in the staff room. A display area of books, curriculum materials, audio- and videotapes clearly marked and catalogued will be appreciated if they are accessible to all staff.

Consider the present use of facilities.

- Are they being used effectively and to their full potential?
- Look at the spaces, are they adequate for present use? Would additional markings make them more appealing to the children or easier for teachers to organise classes and small groups? (Some examples of playground markings are shown in Chapter 5.)
- Would it be possible to acquire additional space from other sources, eg neighbouring primary or secondary schools or the local community? Could a rota system be operated to enhance provision of facilities?
- Are the facilities well maintained? This might be an issue that needs to be raised with the headteacher and governors.

Safety

The most comprehensive book about matters relating to safety in Physical Education is *Safe Practice in Physical Education* (BAALPE, 1995). In many authorities every school was sent a copy from the LEA. Coordinators need to be familiar with the guidance in the text and use it as a reference for guidance about safety in the school. There are, however, certain safety aspects which need to be addressed as a matter of course:

- Equipment needs to be checked annually – this is especially important in the case of gymnastics equipment. Before Local Management of Schools (LMS), this tended to be the responsibility of the LEA. As curriculum coordinator you need to ensure that an annual check is made by an expert and that any defects are reported and dealt with as soon as possible.
- Playing areas – the playground, and fields on or off site – also need to be checked in terms of safety and maintenance. You will need to know who to contact if, for example, you or other members of staff consider that the tarmac is in need of repair, that the grass needs cutting or markings need to be renewed.
- Check the arrangements for first aid both on and off site. All staff should know where to find a first aid box and the whereabouts of a telephone. The school might need to consider establishing a policy whereby any teacher working off-site is accompanied by another adult who would be able to give assistance in the case of an accident.

Shared facilities

It is important that if the school uses a community area, all are able to do so with the minimum of interference from other users. It might be helpful to all concerned if additional markings or boundaries are established to help in the management and organisation of children, this is particularly useful if schools have to share their swimming sessions with members of the public or use a public park for games or athletics activities.

In any policy statement it is important to state roles and responsibilities if the school uses shared facilities. For example, who has responsibility for first aid at the leisure centre? Who has the responsibility for life-saving at the swimming pool?

Interpersonal skills

Enabling leaders not only encourage, they demand that teachers make the fullest contribution to the development of the school in its pursuit of excellence that it is possible to make. Anything else results in second best for pupils. Enabling leaders self-consciously bring to the act of management the highest standards of integrity, responsibility, justice, equality, discipline and love. Further they also have an unfailing belief that this is a requirement of all the members of the school community, not just those with designated leader functions.

(Day, Hall, Gammage and Coles, 1993, p.29)

These authors suggested that you need to be able to create and communicate an enduring vision of what is possible and desirable and to encourage:

● creative thinking and learning;
● colleagues to see themselves as having the ability to contribute effectively to curriculum development.

Analysing the work of Duigan (1987) they identified several factors coordinators need to consider:

● it is essential to foster a climate of trust and openness;
● to plan and work together;
● to remember that those affected by decisions should be involved in making them.

Using a case study approach, Williamson (1984) highlighted some of the problems encountered by curriculum coordinators in Physical Education. These included being unaware of the existing level of competence of individual teachers and not involving all members of staff, especially those with more experience than yourself. Participation by teachers in the decision-making process is essential to effective management. In planning staff development you need to take account of each individual's stage of professional development and design appropriate learning opportunities. Individual and whole staff needs must be considered when managing any change or development.

There is no doubt that effective leadership is dependent on your interpersonal skills and ability to communicate. You need to be sensitive and aware of the strengths and needs of others. Harrison and Theaker (1989) outlined some of the qualities required for effective leadership. You should be able to: **Communicate; Analyse; Plan; Evaluate; Deploy; Persuade; Act** (p.5).

'Most important, then are the skills of working with people. No amount of forward planning, careful budgeting or efficient administration can substitute for this' (Day et al., 1993, p.27).

Tread carefully – take one step at a time

Many people feel ill prepared for the demands of the role which is in addition to all the responsibilities of class teaching. Begin with informal discussions with staff and try to recognise their starting points, strengths and their concerns. You might find that less confident colleagues confide in you and express their worries about certain aspects of teaching Physical Education. Safety and achieving progression are common concerns. Take great care not to intimidate colleagues with your 'superior knowledge'. Over-enthusiastic Physical Education coordinators who have made others feel inadequate have failed to have much impact on the development of the subject in their schools. By all means demonstrate your interest and enthusiasm, but do be sensitive and acknowledge the skills of others. Try to build up a picture of their qualities and strengths, and identify starting points for development. You need to 'create an atmosphere of mutual trust and support, so that curriculum planning and renewal is done within a community of enquiry' (Day et al., 1993).

Organising professional development for colleagues

Physical Education provision may be part of the school development plan: if it is not, it is through formal and informal consultations with colleagues that the focus for professional development provision will evolve. OFSTED (1995a) identified more INSET as a key issue for primary schools, to give teachers the confidence to teach the full National Curriculum in Physical Education at Key Stages 1 and 2.

In planning any support for your school you need to consider the professional learning needs of the staff as individuals and as a whole.

- Endeavour to find out what they feel they need and look for common ground as a starting point.
- The timing of INSET is important. Colleagues will be most receptive to learning if they are not feeling pressures from other commitments.
- An environment must be created which is conducive to professional development.

Remember, 'Successful change only occurs when teachers believe in the need for it, know where it is going, are committed to it and have some ownership of it' (Harrison and Cross, 1994, p.17).

In providing support for colleagues there are a variety of strategies which, as coordinator, you might employ – these include:

- Acting as a critical friend and working alongside individuals.
- Setting up reciprocal and team teaching situations for colleagues.
- Attending local, regional or national courses and reporting back, sharing handouts, ideas and resources.
- Initiating discussion groups for which you set the agendas, chair the meeting and lead the discussions.
- Involving teachers in practical workshops, either working with children or enabling them to be actively involved in practical activities.
- Providing video material for teachers to observe. This might take the form of examples of children's work in your school or professionally produced videos and act as a catalyst for staff discussion (see Chapter 5 for video resources).
- Identifying broader issues to be addressed through the Physical Education programme (eg equality of opportunity, cross-curricular links, health education).
- Coordinating the writing of any curriculum documents to support the teaching and learning of Physical Education .

HMI (DES, 1991c) reported that notes written by coordinators which included advice on lesson planning, the presentation of movement tasks, observation and discussion, criteria for achieving good quality movement and progression, management of materials and class control were considered to be particularly helpful for colleagues.

Formulating a curriculum document for Physical Education

The documentation for the subject will be an indicator of the extent to which the curriculum makes broad, balanced and coherent provision for all aspects of pupils' development (OFSTED, 1995a). Although HMI have recognised that written guidelines do not automatically result in good practice (DES, 1991c), it has long been recommended that schools produce written statements about policy and practice relating to the Physical Education programme. In order to be effective the document should represent a true picture of Physical Education in your school and should not be compiled simply to impress parents, governors or OFSTED. The best documentation evolves over time and has been written as a result of staff discussion under the guidance of the curriculum coordinator (DES, 1991c).

The style and presentation of the curriculum document is a matter of personal choice or it may be determined by school policy. There is no 'official' guidance about what should be included in such a document, however the best examples tend to feature:

- a mission statement or school policy in relation to Physical Education
- aims of Physical Education.

Curriculum coordinators will find the Non-Statutory Guidance helpful here.

The Aims of Physical Education

1.1 Physical Education contributes to the overall education of young people by helping them to lead full and valuable lives through engaging in purposeful physical activity. It can:

- develop physical competence and help to promote physical development;
- teach pupils, through experience, to know about and value the benefits of participation in physical activity while at school and throughout life;
- develop an appreciation of skilful and creative performance across the areas of activity.

1.2 Physical Education can also contribute to:

- the development of problem-solving skills (e.g. by giving pupils the opportunities to make up and refine their own games);
- the establishment of self-esteem through the development of physical confidence (e.g. swimming 25 metres unaided);
- the development of inter-personal skills (e.g. by helping pupils to be aware of their roles as members of teams and groups and taking account of others' ideas).

1.3. Physical activity is combined with thinking involved in making decisions and selecting, refining, judging and adapting movements. Through these activities pupils should be encouraged to develop the personal qualities of commitment, fairness and enthusiasm.

(p.B1)

As coordinator you need to make colleagues aware of these aims and together use them as a basis for discussion in producing aims which are relevant to Physical Education in your school.

Objectives
The school needs to identify what the majority of children will understand and be able to do at the end of each year and Key Stage. The end of Key Stage descriptions describe the types and range of performance that the majority of pupils should characteristically demonstrate by the end of the Key Stage and should be considered in the planning process.

Key Stage 1
Pupils plan and perform simple skills safely, and show control in linking actions together. They improve their performance through practising their skills, working alone and with a partner. They talk about what they and others have done, and are able to make simple judgements. They recognise and describe the changes that happen to their bodies during exercise.

Key Stage 2
Pupils find solutions, sometimes responding imaginatively, to the various challenges that they encounter in the different areas of activity. They practise, improve and refine their performance, and repeat series of movements they have performed previously, with increasing control and accuracy. They make simple judgements about their own and others' performance, and use this information effectively to improve the accuracy, quality and variety of their own performance. They sustain energetic activity over appropriate periods of time, and demonstrate that they understand what is happening to their bodies during exercise. (DFE, 1995a, p.11)

Schemes of work including examples of lessons plans. Statements relating to: The management and organisation of groups and materials and teaching styles –

- **Progression**
- **Assessment, reporting and recording**
- **Cross-curricular links**
- **Equality of opportunity**
- **Partnerships**
- **Resources**

The most useful source of reference for addressing many of these issues is the document *Physical Education for ages 5 to 16* (DES/WO, 1991b).

CHAPTER 3

Managing and Planning the Physical Education Curriculum at Key Stages 1 and 2

Assess the situation

When reviewing the provision of Physical Education in the school it might be helpful to address the following issues in relation to curriculum and assessment. These questions are based on the guidance on inspection requirements of Nursery and Primary Schools (OFSTED, 1995a).

1. Does the curriculum meet the statutory requirements of the National Curriculum for Physical Education?

2. Is adequate time provided for teaching the different components of the Physical Education curriculum?

3. Is there continuity and progression through the Programmes of Study between
   Years
   Key Stages
   Schools?

4. In planning the curriculum have you considered pupils'
   Age
   Attainment
   Gender
   Ethnicity
   Understanding of English
   Special educational needs?

5. Is there an effective system of assessment to plan future work in Physical Education?

6. Are aspects of health education addressed through the Physical Education programme?

7. Is the curriculum enriched by extracurricular activities, including sport?

(The number of each of the above questions corresponds to the numbering of the following sections.)

1. *The statutory requirements of the National Curriculum Order are clearly set out in the document (DFE, 1995a); however, some schools may experience difficulties in implementing the requirements.*

OFSTED (1995a) found that 'Many primary class teachers lack subject knowledge in physical education, and are not confident that they can meet the requirements of the National Curriculum' (p.14). Curriculum coordinators will need to identify INSET needs to support colleagues in curriculum development.

Some schools may be restricted by the facilities. Limited indoor space, badly maintained hard areas or fields, or community halls and playing fields a distance from the school may influence the balance of the activity areas within the National Curriculum. In the survey of good practice *Physical Education and Sport in Schools*, OFSTED (1995c) found that 'facilities still had a major influence on what was taught' (p.13). In an attempt to overcome some of these difficulties schools might consider sharing facilities with other local primary schools or approaching the Physical Education department in the secondary school to see if there are times during the year when it would be possible to use their facilities.

2. *Neither the Department for Education and Employment (DFEE) nor the National Curriculum Council have stipulated the amount of time that should be made available for Physical Education at any Key Stage.*

In the recent survey of good practice by HMI (OFSTED, 1995c), most primary schools had between 8 per cent and 10 per cent of the week devoted to Physical Education. As there is no official guidance on time allocation it would seem sensible to try to secure at least 10 per cent of the timetable for the subject. There needs to be sufficient time to enable pupils to develop competence in each of the Programmes of Study and to achieve the standards required by the End of Key Stage Descriptions.

At Key Stage 1 where only three areas of the curriculum are compulsory, equal weighting could be given to Dance, Gymnastics Activities and Games throughout each year. However if the school decides to offer Swimming in the curriculum it might be necessary to operate a rotation system and block the activities to incorporate

Swimming into the programme.

Year 1	Dance Games Gymnastics	Dance Games Gymnastics	Dance/Gymnastics Games Swimming
Year 2	Gymnastics Games Swimming/Dance	Gymnastics Games Dance	Gymnastics Games Dance

Figure 3.1 Key Stage 1 Programme (including Swimming)

At Key Stage 2 where six areas of activity have to be taught, the Programmes of Study need to be covered by the end of the Key Stage. However, when planning a balanced programme 'it is not necessary for each area of activity to have an equal share of curriculum time' (NCC, 1992, p.C1). Since that guidance was written, the requirements have been made more explicit and only Dance, Gymnastics Activities and Games must be taught in every year through the Key Stage. It is at points during the Key Stage when Athletics Activities, Outdoor and Adventurous Activities and Swimming will be taught. The structure of the programme is a matter of choice for individual schools. An example of whole school planning is provided (see Figure 3.2).

3. *Continuity and progression*

Schools need to plan schemes and units of work to ensure continuity and progression between years, key stages and schools. Communication between coordinators at each Key Stage in primary schools and liaison with the secondary school head of the Physical Education department is important when planning for continuity. Some of the issues about planning for progression within the Programmes of Study are addressed in Chapter 4.

Devising schemes of work

A scheme of work is a written statement which describes the work planned for pupils over a period of time, such as a key stage. It needs to be drawn up using the programmes of study and end of key stage descriptions. The statutory and non-statutory parts of the Order need to be identified, interpreted and developed into structured programmes of learning experiences which are related to the policies, resources and circumstances of individual schools. A scheme of work normally covers a whole key stage but in the case of Key Stage 2 it might be more manageable if a scheme covers half a key stage. Learning activities can be planned in shorter units of work. It is an essential part of each school's responsibility to produce such schemes relating to the teaching of all their pupils.

A scheme of work will need to give details of what is to be taught, how and when it is to be taught, what form of assessment will be used and how the needs of all pupils will be met (Curriculum Council for Wales (CCW), 1992, p.21).

WHOLE SCHOOL PLANNING FOR PHYSICAL EDUCATION

	Autumn		Spring		Summer	
	Activity	*Minutes*	*Activity*	*Minutes*	*Activity*	*Minutes*
Reception	Dance	30	Dance	30	Dance	30
	Games	30	Games	30	Games	30
	Gymnastics	30	Gymnastics	30	Gymnastics	30
Year 1	Dance	30	Dance	30	Dance	30
	Games	30	Games	30	Games	30
	Gymnastics	30	Gymnastics	30	Gymnastics	30
Year 2	Dance	30	Dance	30	Dance	30
	Games	30	Games	30	Games	30
	Gymnastics	30	Gymnastics	30	Gymnastics	30
Year 3	Dance	30	Dance	30	Athletics/ Games	45
	Games	45	Games	45	Gymnastics/ Dance	45
	Gymnastics	45	Gymnastics	45	Swimming	30
Year 4	Dance	40	Swimming	30	Swimming	30
	Games	40	Games	40	Games	40
	Gymnastics	40	Gymnastics /Dance	40	Athletics	40
Year 5	Dance	45	Dance	45	Athletics	45
	Games	45	Games	45	Games	45
	Gymnastics	45	Gymnastics	45	Outdoor & Adventurous Activities	45
Year 6	Dance	45	Dance	45	Athletics	45
	Games	45	Games	45	Games	45
	Gymnastics	45	Gymnastics	45	Outdoor & Adventurous Activities	45

Figure 3.2

Schemes of work reflect the school's long term planning and the schemes should be regularly reviewed and if necessary revised, however this should not be the sole responsibility of the curriculum coordinator. 'Where possible, it should be a collaborative activity carried out by a team of teachers, so that all have a sense of ownership, and the opportunity to develop professionally' (CCW, 1992, p.24).

Both the NCC (1992) and CCW (1992) recommended that the teacher's medium term planning should be represented by units of work and they recognised that the number and duration of units will vary from school to school. The CCW highlighted the variety of ways in which units may be planned and delivered by a school:

• distributed through a weekly timetabled lesson;
• blocked practice, eg swimming each day for three/four weeks;
• as part of a cross-curricular theme, eg dance;
• as a residential experience, eg outdoor and adventurous activities. (p.24)

In planning units of work teachers need to cover the General Requirements and the Programme of Study for the Key Stage. Although the Non-Statutory Guidance documents (NCC, 1992; CCW, 1992) were written to support teachers implementing the 1992 Order (DES, 1991c) and there have been some changes in the requirements since then (see Williams, 1996, for an overview). Teachers planning units of work will find both documents extremely valuable as they each give detailed examples of content and frameworks for planning units of work for each Programme of Study. The example here, Figure 3.3, is adapted from NCC guidance.

Planning for progression
A major challenge for teachers in Primary schools is how to make individual tasks in Physical Education progressive. Take the Programme of Study for Gymnastics Activities for example: at Key Stage 1 pupils should be taught 'different ways of performing the basic actions of travelling using hands and feet, turning, rolling, jumping, swinging and climbing' (p.3), and at Key Stage 2 'different means of turning, rolling, swinging, jumping, climbing, balancing and travelling on hands and feet' (p.4). The basic actions may be presented in a different sequence in the document but the same basic actions are to be taught throughout infant and junior school. It does require fundamental knowledge and understanding and a certain degree of imagination and flair to offer children an inspiring curriculum spanning six years based on the actions of travelling, turning, jumping, balancing, swinging and climbing! Teachers

Figure 3.3 A Framework for Planning a Unit of Work

Programme of Study Area of Activity:		Intended Learning Outcome				
Year:	**Key Stage:**	**Time (no. of lessons):**			**Title of unit:**	
Cross-curricular elements: The unit of work could indicate which elements to include						
Lesson Structure This structure may vary according to area of activity	**Lesson 1**	**Lesson 2**	**Lesson 3**	**Lesson 4**	**Lesson 5**	**Lesson 6**
Introduction						
Development						
Conclusion						
Resources needed:						
General requirements across all key stages:	**End of key stage descriptions** End of key stage descriptions covered by the unit of work	**Criteria for assessing attainment:** Criteria for assessing attainment will need to be devised. Consideration could be given to attainment in: difficulty, quality, independence, interaction				

Adapted from NCC (1992) Physical Education non-statutory Guidance (C9) need to know how to present the curriculum in such a way that it is both challenging and accessible to all pupils. Some ideas towards achieving this are suggested in the section on Gymnastics Activities in Chapter 4.

Although children follow the same pattern of motor development, rates of progression will vary according to age, ability and experience. To ensure progression it is also important that lines of communication between teachers in year groups, between key stages and schools are open. The Non-Statutory Guidance documents (NCC, 1992; CCW, 1992) are very helpful for reference and the NCC document gives some aspects to develop when planning for progression:

- Difficulty
- Quality
- Independence
- Interaction.

Progression in Physical Education involves pupils moving from (see CCW document, p.26).

- dependence to independence in learning;
- performing given tasks to being able to structure their own;
- using given criteria to judge others' performance to develop their own criteria to evaluate their own and others' performance;
- simple tasks to difficult tasks and complex ones;
- natural movements to skilful/artistic technical performance.

In the following chapter these aspects will be considered in relation to the teaching and learning of games, gymnastic activities and dance.

4. *Equality of opportunity*

The Physical Education Working Group (DES, 1991a, p.17) acknow-ledged that certain principles applied to all subject areas: however, it identified several factors to be considered in providing equality of opportunity in Physical Education. They are:

(a) the public nature of success and failure in physical education;
(b) the competitive nature of many physical education activities;
(c) the legacy of single sex teaching and teacher education in physical education;
(d) moves towards mixed sex grouping, sometimes without an educational rationale, and without consideration of the conditions under which mixed sex teaching and single sex teaching might be more successful or appropriate;
(e) the biological and cultural effects of being female or male on the behaviour considered appropriate for girls and boys of different cultures;

(f) the physical nature of physical education, and the emergence of sexuality during key stages 2, 3 and 4, providing both problems and opportunities for physical education in challenging body images, sex stereotypes and other limited perspectives which constrain the choices and achievements of disabled children, and of both girls and boys;

(g) the effects of some culturally restricted interpretations of masculinity on the place and value of dance in the school curriculum, and on boys' opportunities for dance experience and education;

(h) the barriers to young people's involvement caused by the restrictive ways some sports and forms of dance are portrayed and practised;

(i) the rich potential for physical education to transcend categories of race, sex and learning need, through nurturing the value of individual contributions in group situations, and through presenting a wide range of cultural forms and experiences which reflect our multi-cultural society;

(j) the treatment of physical education in the sex discrimination legislation and the varied levels of understanding of its effect on curriculum physical education, extra-curricular activities and school sport.

All those concerned with managing the Physical Education curriculum would also be advised to read 'Equal Opportunity: A Guiding and Leading Principle for Physical Education' (see DES, 1991c). This report, *The Teaching and Learning of Physical Education*, highlighted the need for every school to have a coherent policy on equal opportunities. It distinguished between access and opportunity and warned that although in some schools children appear to have the same access to the curriculum, their opportunity to participate in the different activities may be restricted by the attitude of the teacher, teaching styles, and the structure and interactions within and between groups.

> Working towards equality of opportunity in physical education not only involves widening and ensuring access. It also requires an understanding and appreciation of the range of pupils' responses to femininity, masculinity and sexuality, to the whole range of ability and disability, to ethnic, social and cultural diversity, and the ways in which these relate for children to physical education. (p.15)

The document highlighted the main factors for consideration:

Special Educational Needs The report defined the children who have special needs in Physical Education: 'Since the subject essentially concerns movement, any child who has a movement difficulty can be regarded as having a special need. Such children will include those who have difficulties with hearing instructions, seeing a movement demonstrated, or understanding what is required of them' (p.55). The report also recognised that children who are particularly talented also have special needs in Physical Education and that schools might need to develop partnerships with other agencies to nurture their abilities.

Four principles for a Physical Education programme for children with special educational needs are explained, these included:

- Entitlement
- Accessibility
- Integration
- Appropriateness.

'Entitlement to participation is a fundamental right for all children, and this often requires modifying the activity to meet the resources of the children' (Sugden and Wright, 1996, p.123). In their paper 'Curricular Entitlement and Implementation for all Children' the authors discussed the main issues to be addressed when planning Physical Education for children with developmental coordination disorder (DCD), physiological impairments, and those who have learning, sensory, emotional or behavioural difficulties. They offered very practical advice to teachers, suggested ways to organise groups, and gave examples of how teachers might work in partnership with support staff. Sugden and Wright also addressed in some detail the strategies teachers could use to make the curriculum accessible to all pupils. This included 'learning context adaptation and analysis': they explain that 'teaching is an interactive process; it involves the resources of the child, the activities to be learned and the context in which these are learned' (p.123), and teachers can adapt the context by giving careful thought to different ways of grouping children and modify tasks to enable all children to participate. Their main message is that thorough planning, good organisation and commitment are essential to good professional practice which will present a curriculum which is accessible to all children. 'Diversity in the resources children bring to the movement situation should not be looked upon as threatening or even a challenge, but should be viewed as absolutely normal as indeed they are' (p.129).

Sex and gender 'In Physical Education children have often been grouped according to sex, but teaching and curriculum content have been differentiated according to gender, giving rise to various issues which need to be addressed' (DES/WO, 1991b, (p.57). Those issues included:

- Mixed sex or single sex groupings
- Physical matching for partner work
- Equal value being given to girls' and boys' activities
- Balanced provision of extra curriculum activities for girls and boys.

'Schools will need to include equal opportunities considerations among the criteria by which they select the content of physical education programmes, so that all children have the opportunity to experience a range of physical activities within both National Curriculum physical education and extra-curricular sport' p.58).

Cultural diversity 'We are using the term cultural diversity to embrace the racial, ethnic, cultural, social and religious heritage brought by children to physical education. These factors give rise to a range of shared identities which provide rich opportunities for physical education to be more multicultural. However, they may also be the focus of prejudice, stereotyping and exclusion – which must be challenged' (p.58). Teachers need to:

- Be sensitive to the possible tensions between generations by avoiding putting children in situations where they are in conflict with their parents regarding expectations in Physical Education (see Carroll and Hollinshead, 1993, for case studies on this issue).
- Be aware of the limitations imposed on children if stereotypical attitudes associated with some ethnic groups are left unchallenged.
- Recognise that 'the variety of cultural forms of sport and dance as expressions of heritage, identity and achievement highlights the potential for understanding which stems from sharing and appreciating each others' experiences'.
- Also understand that 'some orthodox religious conventions pose challenges to the full participation of girls in physical activity. The focus of the teacher of physical education should be on how to enable or facilitate girls to take part. Physical activity in itself is rarely a problem but the context and means of delivery will be affected by the religious requirements of some groups. For example, some girls may always have to be taught in single sex groups, by the same sex teachers, in private without onlookers.'
- Be aware that some children will be fasting. 'One of the features of the Islamic religion is the period of Ramadan which lasts for approximately one month. Almost all the Muslim families insist that their children fast from sunrise to sunset during this period, which means the youngsters must go without food and water for the whole of the school day. The problem is that a child can become very tired and strenuous physical exercise can cause discomfort and be distressing' (Carroll and Hollinshead, 1993). Make allowances if necessary.
- Recognise the contribution of Physical Education in making links between involvement in physical activity at school and in the community.

Schools need to have a policy on clothing which meets the requirements of modesty and the religious code and which at the same time considers the comfort and safety of all pupils. This might involve allowing Muslim children to wear tracksuit trousers or a shalwar for Physical Education. However, any policy must meet the needs of all children and should not discriminate in favour of a few.

Obviously all situations will vary. 'While most teachers will agree with the aim of equal opportunities, there will be a range of strategies and practices which can facilitate it. Different strategies will need to be adopted in different schools and different communities' (DES/WO, 1991b, p.60).

5. *Is there an effective system of assessment to plan future work in Physical Education?*

Assessment is an integral part of teaching and learning and schools need to consider a policy on assessment to provide a manageable framework across the curriculum (School Curriculum and Assessment Authority, 1995).

When teaching Physical Education teachers need to consider children's ability to plan, perform and evaluate their own work and the work of others across the Programmes of Study. Throughout their years in Primary school children should be given credit for what they know, understand and can do in the various components of the subject. Too often in the past only those children who were skilled performers were recognised for their abilities, however the National Curriculum has helped us to focus on other dimensions involved in the teaching of Physical Education and to make success in these aspects of the curriculum more accessible to pupils.

So what might we be looking for when making formative assessments about children's work in Physical Education? The guidance offered by Clay (1995) was very helpful here:

Planning You need to consider the way in which children plan before or during performance, the decisions they make in envisioning or anticipating actions, the understanding they display and the effect of their planning on subsequent performance. As children move through the Key Stage good planning involves:

● thinking ahead
● anticipating responses of others
● working cooperatively
● working in pairs and small groups.

Performing Look for appropriate solutions to tasks and the ways in which children find solutions to physical problems. As children move throughout each Key Stage you need to look at the ways in which children perform in each area of activity and consider the extent of their increased competence and versatility. Children should begin to adapt and refine their actions to suit changing circumstances. Other aspects of their performance include their mastery of dynamic qualities, their use of space and their understanding of safety principles.

Evaluating At Key Stage 1 children should be capable of making simple judgements about their own and others' performance and by Key Stage 2 they should be able to observe more accurately. Teachers should take account of the ways in which children evaluate during performance, their skills in observing and comparing and the use they make of the evaluations.

In considering whether teachers assess pupils' work thoroughly and constructively and use assessments to inform teaching, OFSTED inspectors will be collecting evidence of 'how well teachers listen and respond to pupils, encourage and where appropriate praise them, recognise and handle misconceptions, build on their responses and steer them towards new learning or clearer understanding' (OFSTED, 1995b, p.71).

6. *Are aspects of health education addressed through the Physical Education Programme?*

The health related aspects of the Physical Education Programmes of Study permeate all four Key Stages and feature in the End of Key Stage Descriptions. It is during these early years that children can begin to understand the role of physical activity in the promotion of health and fitness. Links with other Programmes of Study where appropriate (for example, Science: 'Life Processes and Living Things', DFE, 1995d) may be developed through the Physical Education Programme to help children to understand humans as organisms, to name the body parts and understand nutrition, circulation and movement. The Physical Education Programme can play a vital role in promoting the physical, social and mental well-being of children.

Bray (1993, p.7) identified some points for consideration:

- Children of primary school age are generally fit and healthy. They inherit many of these attributes and take them for granted.
- In this technological age children have more choices than their forefathers in how to spend their leisure time.

- Children spend a great deal of their leisure time being inactive.
- Children who have enjoyed physical activity are likely to be active adults. Habits and attitudes formed during these early years are often taken into adulthood.
- Children should be taught to understand very simply the effects of exercise on their bodies.

Children should be encouraged to exercise safely. They need to know (i) what to wear, (ii) how to warm up, (iii) what are considered to be undesirable exercises, and (iv) how to cool down.

The Happy Heart Project, Health Education Authority (1990) and Sleap (1995) offer teachers practical ideas for promoting health in Physical Education. Armstrong and Bray (1991), and Sleap and Warburton (1992), have studied primary children's physical activity patterns and stressed the need for children to be introduced to a variety of enjoyable activities to stimulate them to be involved in more physical activity to enhance their health when they have choices.

If the Physical Education programme is well planned and coherent and offers children enjoyable and worthwhile experiences which help them to develop confidence and skill and a positive feeling of well being, then the likelihood is that children will choose to engage in physical activity in their leisure time. This in turn will contribute to healthy lifestyles and lay the foundations for lifetime participation in physical activity.

7. Extra curricular activities

It might come as a surprise to some teachers to realise that 'Inspectors must inspect and report on the quality, time spent and range of games offered as part of the physical education curriculum and on the provision of sport outside formal lessons, paying particular attention to traditional team games. Reports should include pupil participation rates in extra-curricular sport, the number of teachers who supervise this activity, sports competitions within and between schools and any improvements the school has made in providing both curricular and extra-curricular competitive games' (OFSTED, 1995a, p.78). This does reflect the present Government's enthusiasm for school sport and competitive team games and is a result of proposals set out in the document *Sport – Raising the Game* (Department of National Heritage, 1995). The proposed Sportsmark system will be awarded to schools offering at least four hours each week of structured sport outside formal lessons which might be during break-times, after school or at weekends. This is not to say that in Primary schools children should be playing full-sided games but sports played 'in a form judged appropriate for the year group by the relevant sports governing body' (p.13). The scheme is scheduled to be set up for Primary schools in the academic year 1997/98.

CHAPTER 4

Planning for Progression and Quality in Games, Gymnastics Activities and Dance

To enable children to achieve high standards teachers need to 'develop coherence out of apparently discrete activities so that pupils can operate competently and confidently across the whole of the Physical Education curriculum' (DES/WO, 1991b, p.9). A coordinated approach to teaching and learning in the subject will ensure that children make sense of the concepts, develop skills in a range of interrelated activities and understand the contribution of physical activity towards achieving a healthy life.

Teachers need to be sensitive to the public nature of performance in Physical Education and use strategies to enable all children to achieve success in the subject without ever having to experience humiliation or a sense of failure.

The learning of physical skill is central to Physical Education: however, teachers also need to remember that 'Children who are required to make few decisions for themselves and who merely respond to instructions are likely to acquire accurate physical skills but are unlikely to develop adaptability or independence' (DES/WO, 1991, p.9).

[Physical Education] is achieved through the combination of physical activity with the mental processes of

- making decisions
- selecting
- refining
- judging
- shaping
- adjusting and adapting.

This process is common to all the Programmes of Study at Key Stages 1 and 2. It should also involve the development of qualities such as commitment, integrity, fairness, enthusiasm and concern for quality as well as success. Thinking, reasoning, observing, planning and judging are as vital to success in a physical context as in any other. Judgements are made and effects assessed before, during and after activity. In this way understanding and appreciation are developed, enabling subsequent actions to be refined and improved, while at the same time allowing pupils to experience the fun, enjoyment and satisfaction that result from successful endeavour (DES/WO, 1991b, p.5).

The challenge for all teachers is to create stimulating learning conditions using a variety of appropriate teaching styles to enable all children to benefit. Observation is the key to good teaching in Physical Education. The transitory nature of movement puts demands on all those concerned with helping children to achieve high quality performance. This chapter will go some way to help less experienced teachers recognise and develop good quality in children's work.

Both teachers and pupils need observational skills to recognise, check, analyse and alter aspects of performance and there should be carefully planned progression if fluency, mastery and individual responsibility for developing skilfulness and creativity are to be achieved.

(DES/WO, 1991b.)

Children learn in Physical Education by:

- Watching demonstrations by the teacher, each other, and through viewing videos of their own or others' work. They benefit from guidance by the teacher every step of the way, for this reason teachers need to know what to look for and how to help children to describe what they see.
- Receiving positive and constructive feedback to help them to improve performance.
- Having the opportunity to evaluate their own and others' work against criteria given by the teacher.
- Having plenty of time to practice and refine performance.
- Working alone, or together in pairs and small groups, sharing ideas and helping each other to plan and improve performance.
- Achieving success through differentiated tasks.
- Experiencing an enjoyable programme which is appropriate to their need.

Teachers generally welcome guidance in planning for progression and the guidance from the DES (1991b) advised that when setting tasks for children teachers need to take into account:

- their level of physical development;
- the stage of cognitive, emotional and social development they have reached;
- the stage they have reached in the process of learning practical skills;
- the level of complexity of the practical skills necessary for each activity.

The DES further reminded us that different children will progress at different rates in relation to each of these categories. Levels of physical maturity are particularly critical in a subject with significant practical content. The extensive variation in such progression amongst children should be carefully noted. To enable children to achieve at their own level, the learning process may be set:

- at different levels of difficulty in relation to each task; or
- as a common task for all children allowing for differentiated outcomes from different children (see DES/WO, 1991b, p.42).

This chapter gives special consideration to some of these factors through Games, Gymnastics Activities and Dance, and the Programmes of Study which need to be taught each year throughout Key Stages 1 and 2. It is acknowledged that at Key Stage 2 children will also be taught Athletic Activities, Outdoor and Adventurous Activities and Swimming at points during the Key Stage and resources to support planning in these Programmes of Study are referred to in Chapter 5.

The National Curriculum guidance provides a structure for planning programmes and it relates to children's natural physical, cognitive and social development. Assessment is an integral part of teaching and learning: to help teachers form some judgements about children's knowledge, skills and understanding in Games, Gymnastics Activities and Dance, some guidance is offered at the end of each section and relates to the Programme of Study and the End of Key Stage Descriptions.

Games at Key Stages 1 and 2

The Programmes of Study for Games are stated:

Key Stage 1
Pupils should be taught:
(a) simple competitive games, including how to play them as individuals and, when ready, in pairs and in small groups;
(b) to develop and practise a variety of ways of sending (including throwing, striking, rolling and bouncing), receiving and travelling with a ball and other similar games equipment;

(c) elements of games play that include running, chasing, dodging, avoiding, and awareness of space and other players.

(DFE, 1995, p.3)

Key Stage 2

Pupils should be taught:

(a) to understand and play small-sided games and simplified versions of recognised competitive team and individual games, covering the following types – invasion (mini-soccer, netball); striking/fielding (rounders, small-sided cricket); net/wall (short tennis);

(b) common skills and principles, including attack and defence in invasion, striking/fielding, net/wall and target games;

(c) to improve the skills of sending, receiving, striking and travelling with a ball in the above games.

(DFE, 1995a, p.4)

A good quality Games programme is well coordinated and well resourced. It enables all children to develop skills and understanding by participating in a variety of enjoyable activities. It should be accessible to all children and boys and girls should be given equal opportunities to experience and achieve success in the activities. Planning for differentiation in Games might include modifying the equipment to make tasks easier (using a large stationary ball to send into play in a striking/fielding game), to making tasks more difficult (hitting a small ball with a rounders bat which has been bowled by a bowler to send into play in a striking/fielding game). Or setting easier tasks (kicking a stationary ball at a target), or more difficult problems for children to solve (receiving a ball on the move, or to aim at a target which is defended by a player). Alternatively differentiation will be achieved by outcome where a common task is set and children perform at different levels of ability. It is often helpful to children in Games activities if they are grouped according to ability. For more explicit examples of planning for differentiation see Non-Statutory Guidance documents NCC (1992) and CCW (1992).

The games equipment should be well maintained and there should be a plentiful supply to allow for whole class teaching (a bat and ball for each child in the class, a skipping rope each). A well taught Games programme should give children the knowledge, skills and confidence to take part in extracurricular sport both at school and in the community. It should also offer children opportunities to:

● explore and experiment with a range of games equipment to develop manipulative skills;

- develop the ability to change pace and direction through a variety of running and chasing games;
- develop and maintain cardiovascular fitness, strength, endurance and flexibility;
- understand the basic principles and some tactics in invasion games, net games and striking/fielding games;
- make decisions and plan together as a team;
- work cooperatively and engage in competitive situations;
- understand the need for rules;
- evaluate their own and others' performance;
- develop self-confidence through successful participation.

Activity
Discuss and evaluate the Games provision in the school. Look at the provision of games equipment. Is it well maintained? Could this be improved? Are the facilities adequate? Could they be enhanced by working in partnership with another school or sharing facilities in the community? Is there a scheme of work for games? Is it used? Could it be updated?

Some general issues relating to Games need to be discussed by all those concerned with teaching the Programme before schemes and units of work are produced. These discussions should also involve people who might be involved with extracurricular provision. The place of competition in the school needs to be considered in the light of the statutory requirements: 'simple competitive games as individuals, in pairs and in small groups' (p.3) at Key Stage 1; to 'small-sided games and simplified versions of recognised competitive team and individual games' (p.4) at Key Stage 2.

Activity
Discuss:

- How does an individual play a competitive game? What form might such a game take?
- Ideas for simple competitive games which would be suitable for infants working

  - as individuals
  - in pairs
  - in small groups.

> • What opportunities could be offered by the school to enable children to enjoy competitive experiences within the school, locally or nationally? Consider what activities would be appropriate, the form of the competition and the structures which might be set up to enable children to have equality of opportunity to take part, for example: How could teams be selected? Would groups be mixed or single sex? Mixed ability or selected for talent?
> • Identify local/national networks for contacts.

Planning the Games curriculum

Thorpe (1990) highlighted four fundamental factors to be considered when developing a Games curriculum. As it is not possible to offer every game within the curriculum, 'sampling will be necessary'. Those concerned with planning the programme need to accept that premise and identify the games forms which will be taught to each year group. He suggested that the technical complexity of the game should be taken into account and reminds us that it is not unusual for more complex invasion games to be the first games to be introduced to children in the Primary phase. He questioned the value of such an approach which he argued does not make sound educational sense if we are endeavouring to help children to develop a knowledge and understanding of games. The logical progression would be to introduce simple net games before more complex invasion team games are attempted. In adapting adult games to make them more accessible to children Thorpe suggested 'modification for representation', that is, mini-hockey, or 'modification by exaggeration', which is illustrated by examples such as changing the size of a badminton court to a long thin playing space to accentuate the long and short aspects of play within the game. This equates well with National Curriculum requirements for children to be taught small-sided and simplified versions of recognised games.

Williamson (1993) provided a sound framework for planning the Games programme and all those concerned with shaping a programme in schools will find this advice useful.

Stage 1 Identify the main principles of play of the three groups of games, allowing for differences between individual games within the group (netball and rugby are both invasion games using space but in different ways).

Stage 2 As far as possible place each principle in order of priority for teaching purposes (eg the simple exploitation of space on a tennis or badminton court is likely to be taught before the idea (short/long placement or use of angles).

Stage 3 Place this order of teaching in a 'timeline' (eg principles to be covered in year 2 will be less sophisticated than those in year 5).

Stage 4 Identify appropriate games and practices which will help children to learn the principles of play (eg 4 versus 3 games to encourage the use of the 'extra' player, or changing the size of the target to encourage pupils to make decisions about appropriate attacking and defensive tactics).

Stage 5 Identify the specific skills/techniques they will need to learn in order to take part in the games/practices at an appropriate level (eg less able pupils learning about 'hitting to spaces', in fielding/striking games they may need to use longer bats and throw and hit a ball themselves, or even simulate the hitting by an underarm roll or throw; more able pupils may be able to cope with a bowler or pitcher with regulation equipment. For these pupils the skills required are more extensive and sophisticated).

Stage 6 The written scheme of work should indicate that the main purpose of teaching is to help pupils understand principles of play and tactics. Techniques and skills are used as a means to achieve this end in the context of the game. They still have to be taught but when the need arises, eg when a pupil or teacher recognises the need to learn or teach a particular skill in order for the player to take part in the game more effectively.

(Avon LEA Module 3 Games 13)

Following the advice of Williamson (1993) to identify the common principles in each games category some suggestions are offered here.

Net games Some of the principles which can be applied to modified games of badminton, newcombe, tennis and volleyball include:

Sending The 'ball' could be a beanbag, quoit, beachball or shuttlecock. Children need to develop the ability to send the ball

● with accuracy, varying the force, speed and direction, into a space on the court to outwit an opponent: in the early stages this might involve throwing the ball into play, progressing to using a racquet;

● make decisions about where to move after sending the ball.

Receiving Watch the ball from the moment it is sent and anticipate where it might land to move to return the pass.

Children need to understand that if they are in possession of the ball, they are attacking, and when receiving they are defending. Spatial awareness is very important in net games and children need to understand that when they are attacking they need to look for spaces on the court into which to return the ball using long/short, high/low passes. They need to know that defenders need to position themselves on court to cover as much of the area as effectively as possible.

Striking/fielding games Some of the principles which can be applied to adapted games of baseball, cricket, rounders, softball and stoolball include:

Bowling Children need to develop the ability to control the force, speed and direction when sending the ball and notice whether the batters are right or left handed.

Batting
- watch the ball from the bowler's hand and judge the force, speed and direction of the ball;
- vary the strength and angle of the hitting action;
- send the ball into undefended spaces;
- make decisions about running.

Fielding
- be alert and ready to receive the ball;
- throw accurately and effectively;
- cover and cooperate with other team members to retrieve the ball.

Children also need to understand that success in striking/fielding games is dependent upon their ability to look for and defend spaces. They need to be given plenty of opportunities to make decisions and exploit situations to practice these skills.

Invasion Games Some of the principles of invasion games which can be applied to simplified versions of football, basketball, hockey, lacrosse, water polo include:

Travelling with the ball
- controlling the ball whilst they are stationary or on the move;
- scanning the area whilst keeping control of the ball;
- creating scoring opportunities by moving close to the target or goal.

Sending the ball
- knowing when to pass the ball and to whom to send it;
- controlling the force, direction and timing of the pass.

Receiving the ball
- creating spaces to receive a pass;

Key Stage 2, Games, Year 6, Invasion game

- signalling for a pass;
- supporting other team players to create all-round passing opportunities;
- spreading out in the space to create width and depth in attack;
- endeavouring to create opportunities to enable one team member to be unmarked to attack the 'goal'.

Defending Knowing how to mark a player or defend an area (for example in person to person marking defenders need to keep close to their attacker when near the goal; when the opposition are attacking the most effective position for the defender is between the attacker and the goal).

Children need to know and understand that all invasion games involve
- two teams;
- playing within boundaries;

and to realise that
- each team has a goal area;
- the aim of the game is to score goals against each other;
- that players' roles change from attack to defence within the game, depending on which team is in possession at the time.

Teachers need to be imaginative in setting up practical activities to help children understand the principles being taught. The best way of doing this is to teach them in a games context.

Cooper has written schemes of work for Games at Key Stage 1 (1995) and Key Stage 2 (1993). Each year scheme includes practical activities and advice on management and organisation. Anyone looking for a structured and progressive course in games skills will find these publications very helpful in formulating their own scheme. In the guidance for the Key Stage 2 curriculum Cooper (1993) has offered practical advice in achieving progression through the programme:

Progression in net games
- begin with cooperative rallying using depth and width and then progress to the use of short and long areas of the court;
- progress to using a variety of different shots (drop, lob and volleys) to teach individual and defensive strategies.

Progression in striking/fielding games
- begin with the bowler and the batter cooperating before they work in competition with each other (for example, the ball is bowled sympathetically to enable the batter to make contact and send the ball into play);
- progress to small-sided games (that is, batter and bowler and 2 fielders)
  - 3 versus 1
  - 4 versus 4
  - 5 versus 5.

Progression in invasion games
- simple games with the emphasis on attacking skills before defending skills, then devise situations to combine both;
- unequal sides before equal sides to allow attacking players to succeed;
- defensive strategies which begin with marking the player with the ball, progress to person-to-person marking and then teach zone defence as a more advanced skill.

Curriculum coordinators planning the Games curriculum across Key Stages 1 and 2 might find the following representation of progression through the Programme a useful source of reference.

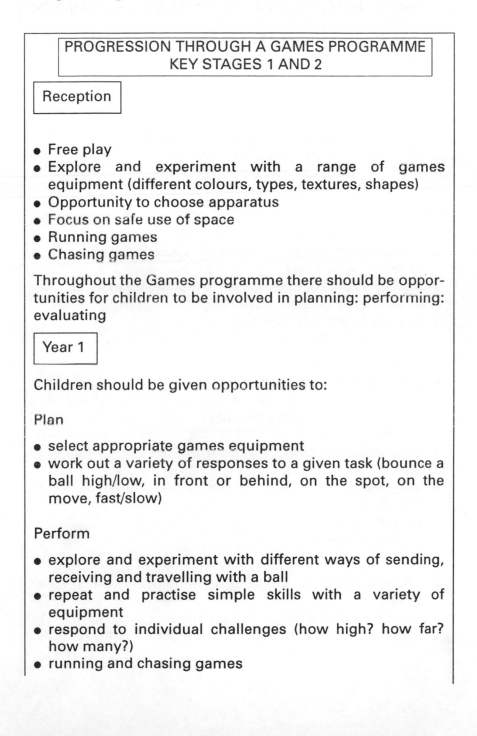

PROGRESSION THROUGH A GAMES PROGRAMME KEY STAGES 1 AND 2

Reception

- Free play
- Explore and experiment with a range of games equipment (different colours, types, textures, shapes)
- Opportunity to choose apparatus
- Focus on safe use of space
- Running games
- Chasing games

Throughout the Games programme there should be opportunities for children to be involved in planning: performing: evaluating

Year 1

Children should be given opportunities to:

Plan

- select appropriate games equipment
- work out a variety of responses to a given task (bounce a ball high/low, in front or behind, on the spot, on the move, fast/slow)

Perform

- explore and experiment with different ways of sending, receiving and travelling with a ball
- repeat and practise simple skills with a variety of equipment
- respond to individual challenges (how high? how far? how many?)
- running and chasing games

Evaluate

- watch a demonstration and with guidance from the teacher identify the good features (catching–watching the ball, reaching out to grasp and secure)
- recognise and describe improvement in own performance

Plan

- work out a variety of solutions to a given task
- select appropriate games equipment
- plan a simple game with another child

Perform

- explore and experiment with selected apparatus
- practise and refine the skills of sending, receiving and travelling with a ball
- create and play simple games in leading up to net games, invasion games, striking/fielding games, target games
- running and chasing games

Evaluate

- describe their own made up games
- with guidance from the teacher recognise and describe features of successful attempts in sending, receiving and travelling skills
- know some changes that occur to their body when they exercise
- recognise the short-term effects of exercise on the body

Years 3 and 4

Plan

- select responses to a task as an individual in pairs, small groups
- plan simple tactics to outwit an opponent
- suggest ways to help a partner in a games context

Perform

- develop and improve personal performance in sending/receiving and travelling with a ball in games-like contexts
- explore and be guided to an understanding of the common skills and principles including attack and defence in net games, invasion games, striking/fielding games
- create simple games individually, in pairs and small groups to practise skills in a games-like context
- running and chasing games

Evaluate

- observe and describe combination of actions (dribble, shoot, retrieve) and describe the pattern of movement
- identify when skills have been used effectively in a games context

Years 5 and 6

Plan

- plan individual and group games activities using appropriate equipment, skills and strategies
- apply simple concepts of attack and defence to net games, invasion games and striking/fielding games

Perform

- demonstrate an understanding of attacking and defending principles in simple small-sided games
- consolidate principles of play and tactics through simplified versions of recognised and made up games
- cooperate and compete in small-sided games
- sustain energetic activity as appropriate

Evaluate

- make judgements about their own work and the work of others and use their observations to improve personal performance
- recognise and describe effective tactics in simple games
- understand the short-term effects of exercise on the body

58

Devon Curriculum Advice (1994) have produced guidelines to support teachers in helping children understand simple tactical concepts and strategies. Their model for teaching games (see Figure 4.1) outlines the process which represents current thinking and best practice in Games education and encapsulates the approaches advocated by Almond (1989), Thorpe (1990), Williamson (1993), Spackman, Collin and Kibble (1995). The following guidance is given by Devon Curriculum Advice (p.76).

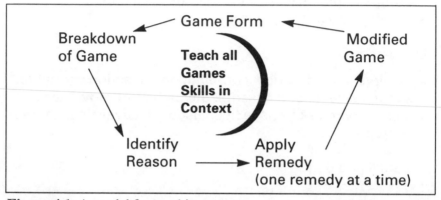

Figure 4.1 A model for teaching games

1. Equipment inappropriate	*Ask children to choose more appropriate equipment (larger ball, lighter/smaller bat).*
2. No defined 'pitch' or playing area	*Make a defined playing area.*
3. No rules, or inappropriate rules	*Select appropriate rules. (How does your game start? What happens when the ball goes out?)*
4. Skill/technique lacking	*Work on developing/improving skills.*
5. Little understanding	*Help develop understanding. (Where is the best place to send the ball?)*
6. Players inappropriately matched	*Match players (in terms of skill, friendship).*

The significance is that children are encouraged to play a game first rather than learn skills first.

Devon Curriculum Advice suggested the following lesson pattern (p.77) for developing a quality Games programme at Key Stage 2 and Key Stage 3:

Warm-up Lesson related activity to raise the heart rate
Modified game Games-related activity which sets the scene for investigating a games principle, such as a scoring game (attacking a target)
Skill practice Selection of one or more skills to practise, related to the learning intention
Modified game Games-related activity which may be a repeat of that used earlier in the lesson or a development to test understanding and skills
Cool-down Activity to reduce heart rate and to settle group.

Coordinators considering assessment might find the following guidelines useful.

ASSESSMENT – GAMES   KEY STAGE 1

Consider

(i)   Performing
(ii)   Planning
(iii) Evaluating
(iv) Health-related exercise

(i) Performing

Identify the simple skills the child is able to perform:

Using balls and other similar games equipment
SENDING ie THROWING STRIKING ROLLING BOUNCING
RECEIVING ie STOPPING TRAPPING CATCHING
TRAVELLING ie USING FEET HANDS GAMES EQUIPMENT

To what extent is the child able to:

- play simple games alone and with others
  - use space, change direction, dodge and avoid others, when working in a group, with and without equipment
  - manipulate equipment effectively
- show control in linking actions together
  - consider body management and control of equipment when performing simple skills (sending the ball to a target, retrieving it to repeat)
- work safely
  - alone

- in pairs
- in groups
- landing and controlling equipment

(ii) Planning

- Plan simple skills
  - consider responses to tasks
  - ability to set personal challenges
  - ability to make decisions (about where to move to receive the ball, where to send it)
  - ability to plan simple moves to outwit opponents alone/in pairs/with groups

(iii) Evaluating

- describe in simple terms what they and others have done in games activities
  - observational skills
  - consider use of language
  - ability to demonstrate their own game or activity

(iv) Health-related exercise

- recognise any changes that happen to the body during exercise
  - in running and chasing games in the warm-up
  - in concluding activities for cool-down

ASSESSMENT – GAMES   KEY STAGE 2

Consider

(i)   Performing
(ii) Planning
(iii) Evaluating
(iv) Health-related exercise

(i) Performing

Identify the basic skills the child is able to perform:

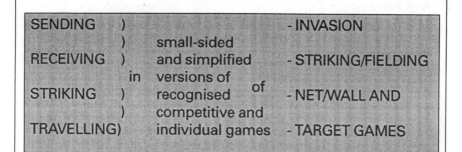

```
SENDING     )                        - INVASION
            )    small-sided
RECEIVING   )    and simplified      - STRIKING/FIELDING
          in     versions of
STRIKING    )    recognised   of     - NET/WALL AND
            )    competitive and
TRAVELLING) individual games         - TARGET GAMES
```

To what extent is the child able to:

- practise, improve and refine performance
  - consider accuracy in the basic skills
  - perseverance with the tasks
  - apply common skills and principles, including attack and defence to each games category
- work safely alone, in pairs and in groups
  - use space, control the ball/bean bag, avoid physical contact with others when moving together

(ii) Planning

- find solutions, sometimes responding imaginatively to various challenges
  - improvise and experiment with different pieces of equipment
  - create games using and applying simple skills
  - cooperate with a partner or team to apply principles to outwit opponents

(iii) Evaluating

- make simple judgements about their own and others' performance
  - acknowledge the contribution an individual will make to a team effort
  - recognise the strengths and weaknesses of others

(iv) Health-related exercise

- take some responsibility for warming-up and cooling-down activities by creating games which adhere to sound principles
  - sustain vigorous activity during warm-up sessions

The Programmes of Study for Gymnastics Activities are stated:

Key Stage 1

Pupils should be taught (p.3):

(a) different ways of performing the basic actions of travelling using hands and feet, turning, rolling, jumping, balancing, swinging and climbing, both on the floor and using apparatus;

Key Stage 1 Gymnastics, Year 2, Jumping for height

(b) to link a series of actions both on the floor and using apparatus, and how to repeat them.

Key Stage 2
Pupils should be taught (p.4):

(a) different means of turning, rolling, swinging, jumping, climbing, balancing and travelling on hands and feet, and how to adapt, practise and refine these actions, both on the floor and using apparatus;
(b) to emphasise changes of shape, speed and direction through gymnastic actions;
(c) to practise, refine and repeat a longer series of actions, making increasingly complex movement sequences, both on the floor and using apparatus.

A good quality Gymnastics programme will have a positive effect on children's physical resources, in particular upper body strength and flexibility. It will provide opportunities to develop refined body management skills, compositional skills and observational skills and help children to gain a better understanding of the body's response to exercise. An effective programme is well planned and taught with regard to progression. This will be achieved through a collaborative approach to planning and teachers making progressive demands on children from lesson to lesson and sometimes within lessons. Progression can be considered in relation to variety, the degree of difficulty and the quality of the work. Another feature is the ability of children to move towards independent decision-making. So, in a good quality Gymnastics programme teachers will endeavour to extend:

• the physical challenge (in terms of difficulty and quantity – from single actions to linked phrases);
• the variety of each pupil's movement vocabulary;
• the quality of movement (control, clarity in body shape, resilience, smooth transitions between actions);
• the number and type of judgements and decisions required of the children.

Throughout the programme the aesthetic aspect of movement will underpin the planning and teachers and children constantly work for high quality execution of all movements or positions no matter how technically simple or difficult they may be, including poised sitting, standing and walking. Children will be helped to structure imaginative sequences which reflect a harmonious blending of body actions in which the recovery from one movement becomes the preparation for the next. They are encouraged to take a pride in their work and have opportunities to observe each other's movements from a qualitative viewpoint. This requires the teacher to help children to develop a vocabulary with which to describe movement and to guide them to recognise good features of their own and others' work.

The good quality Gymnastics programme is taught in such a way that it enables all children to feel successful and to enjoy gymnastics. This puts

Key Stage 2 Gymnastics, Year 6, Clarity of body shape

demands on teachers to plan for differentiation and to praise children for their achievements in planning, performing and evaluating. If children know that their work is valued, self-confidence and self-esteem will be enhanced. Improved poise and coordination and feelings of success in response to a variety of challenges will go a long way towards helping to develop a positive self image. The programme will also give children opportunities to develop their social skills and to cooperate with others:

- in designing sequences;
- carrying and arranging apparatus;
- performing in pairs, groups;
- evaluating others' performance;

and to be sensitive to the needs and achievement of others.

Some teachers express concerns about teaching Gymnastics and have difficulty in analysing movement and knowing how to encourage children to develop basic actions into high quality Gymnastics Activities. Answering the questions, What?, How?, Where?, In what context?, can be helpful here.

Identify the actions which are being demonstrated – travelling, rolling, balancing, jumping, swinging and climbing. Look for technical competence, originality and variety of interpretation. Having identified the activity content of the work it may be developed through a focus on spatial or dynamic qualities.

Look at the way in which the actions are performed. Is there controlled use of body tension, for example in balancing and in holding body shape in action? Look for resilience in landing and rolling. Study the movement to see if children are moving freely so that one movement moves harmoniously and naturally into the next.

Consider timing in the performance. Some movements naturally occur quickly and others are enhanced when performed slowly. Contrasts in speed can add interest and surprise to the work. Gymnastic activities may be performed rhythmically and continuously, others benefit from being punctuated by moments of stillness. In developing children's work consider contrasts in speed to enhance performance.

> Analyse the use of space. Encourage children to develop maximum use of space in front, above, behind and to the side, using a variety of body shapes, long, wide, twisted, curved, symmetrical and asymmetrical. Consider floor and aerial pathways forwards, backwards, sideways, upwards and downwards.

> Analyse the best setting for the child to develop the work. Consider individual work, working in pairs, in groups; with or without apparatus, with or without music.

Worries about safety when teaching Gymnastics are common and there is no doubt that Gymnastics should be taught with constant reference to safety.

- A disciplined working atmosphere needs to be established to help children to concentrate. This is not to say children should work in silence but the level of conversation should be such that the teacher is able to attract the attention of the whole class at once to watch a demonstration or listen to an instruction.
- The movement material selected should be appropriate to the skill level, previous experience, physical and temperamental resources of the children.
- When giving children open-ended tasks it might be necessary to set some restrictions to ensure their safety (for example, if you ask children to find different ways of turning whilst travelling towards and away from the apparatus you would tell them that somersaults in the air off the box are unsafe).
- There needs to be a whole school policy for the safe storage and use of apparatus so that children know that as they move from class to class the rules are the same for correct lifting and carrying, erecting and dismantling apparatus. Children must not be allowed to move on any apparatus until it has been checked for safety by the teacher. Check that all bolts are secure, all hooks are correctly in place and that mats have been placed in a position where pupils can safely dismount from the apparatus without interfering with another group or bumping into apparatus, chairs, piano, walls or radiators.
- Apparatus, including mats, must be properly positioned for safe use; heights should be carefully selected in relation to pupil competence.

A very useful video and booklet is available which focuses on this aspect (*Safe Use of Apparatus*, Birmingham City Council, 1993). This could form the starting point for staff discussions at an INSET meeting. See also *Safe Practice in Physical Education* (BAALPE, 1995).

There is no one way to deliver the programme. In the early years teachers will be building on children's natural love of movement and concentrating on safe use of space and body awareness. Whereas at Key Stage 2 children will tend to work in groups on apparatus and rotate to each arrangement during a unit of work, there might be times in Key Stage 1 when teachers might feel it is appropriate to allow children to move freely from one piece of apparatus to another – gaining confidence and exploring the space.

There are many schemes of work which have been written to help teachers deliver progressive and well-balanced programmes of Gymnastics Activities (see Chapter 5). Most guidance advocates developing units of work related to a theme or focus. These may be adopted by the school as a basis for individual planning. When planning schemes of work, identify the aspects of planning, performing and evaluating to be developed.

Planning This involves children in designing their own sequences. They will need opportunities to:

- explore and improvise and select ideas through movement;
- make decisions, solve problems and select appropriate movement content alone or with others;
- share their ideas with others through practical demonstration or discussion;
- practice and refine single actions and sequences of movement;
- understand simple compositional structures (copying, mirroring, contrasting, performing with a group in canon or unison).

Performing This involves children developing, practising and refining gymnastic activities. They will need time and opportunity to:

- develop the skills of travelling, turning, jumping, balancing, swinging and climbing;
- develop the ability to link actions together, with control and smooth transitions;
- practice, refine and repeat actions;
- develop the ability to use space safely, alone and with others, with changes in direction and level;

- vary the speed in gymnastic action;
- show clarity in body shape, in balance and in action;
- be able to cooperate and work with a partner or group.

Evaluating This involves children describing their own work or the work of others. They need to be able to:

- recognise the content of the performance;
- develop a vocabulary to describe gymnastic activities;
- observe carefully and recognise different shapes, pathways, changes of speed;
- describe in simple terms the compositional features of sequences;
- evaluate their own and others' performance.

In addition curriculum coordinators planning the Gymnastics Activities programme across Key Stages 1 and 2 might find the following representation of progression through the programme a useful source for reference.

PROGRESSION THROUGH A GYMNASTICS ACTIVITIES PROGRAMME KEY STAGES 1 AND 2

Reception

- Explore a variety of ways to travel on feet, hands and feet, turn, roll, jump and land safely
- Focus on safe use of space and awareness of others' work, on travelling and stopping, changing direction
- Explore a variety of apparatus – travel on and around, swing, climb and balance

Year 1

Children should be given opportunities to:

Plan

- explore and select responses to tasks
- solve simple problems (can you travel on two hands and one foot with tummy facing the floor?)

Perform

- explore a variety of ways to travel on feet, hands and feet, turn, roll, jump and land safely with same control
- balance on wide and narrow bases
- transfer some of the basic actions performed on the floor to low surfaces (travel on and around large apparatus, swing, climb and balance)

Evaluate

- talk about their work and the gymnastic actions of others

Year 2

Plan

- plan simple sequences individually and in pairs in response to tasks
- help to arrange apparatus with guidance from the teacher

Perform

- link actions together to form short sequences individually and when ready in pairs
- practise, repeat and refine performance
- vary the speed and direction and use of space and levels in performance

Evaluate

- talk about what they and others have done, identifying key features through guidance by the teacher
- make simple judgements about content and quality of performance, and the cooperative work when working together in pairs.

Years 3 and 4

Plan

- find solutions to tasks
- design imaginative sequences individually, in pairs or small groups

Perform

- practice and refine the basic actions of travelling, turning, rolling, jumping, climbing and balancing
- remember and perform more complex sequences of movements on the floor and apparatus
- add variety to performance through change of shape, speed and direction

Evaluate

- describe their own and others' performance and make comments on use of space, clarity of body shape in stillness and in action
- talk about the composition of the sequence (the fluency of the movement, the use of floor and aerial pathways and changes in level)
- make comment on changes of speed and dynamics in the work observed

Years 5 and 6

Plan

- solve simple problems individually, in pairs, in small groups
- plan and compose more complex sequences of movement
- design apparatus layouts appropriate to the task

Perform

- longer and more complex sequences of movement
- practice and refine performance, demonstrating clarity in body shape in stillness and in action, smooth transitions between elements of the sequences
- imaginative use of space, floor and apparatus
- changes of dynamics in movement, including changes in speed and tension
- alone, with a partner and in groups

Evaluate

- describe and reflect on solutions to tasks
- discuss decisions made when working in pairs and groups
- comment on the quality of work observed in relation to content, performance, compositional design

---

ASSESSMENT – GYMNASTICS ACTIVITIES
KEY STAGE 1

Consider

   (i)   Performing
   (ii) Planning
   (iii) Evaluating
   (iv) Health-related exercise

(i) Performing

Identify the basic actions the child is able to perform:

On floor and apparatus
TRAVELLING   TURNING   ROLLING   JUMPING
(using hands
and feet)
                 BALANCING

On apparatus
          SWINGING   CLIMBING

To what extent is the child able to:

- perform simple skills
  - consider control
  - clarity in body shape
  - use of space
  - resilience in both landing and rolling activities on the floor and on apparatus

- show control in linking actions together
  - consider coordination

- smooth transitions between action
- use of different directions, levels and changes of speed in movement sequences

● work safely
  - alone
  - in pairs
  - in groups
  - lifting and handling apparatus

(ii) Planning

● plan simple skills
  - consider responses to tasks
  - range of movement vocabulary
  - creativity in planning sequences
  - ability to perform the planned activity

(iii) Evaluating

● describe in simple terms what they and others have done through gymnastic activities
  - consider observational skills
  - use of language
  - written work
  - art work

(iv) Health-related exercise

● recognise and describe the changes that happen to the body during exercise

---

ASSESSMENT – GYMNASTICS ACTIVITIES KEY STAGE 2

Consider:

    (i)   Performing
    (ii) Planning
    (iii) Evaluating
    (iv) Health-related exercise

(i) Performing

Identify the basic actions the child is able to perform:

On floor and apparatus
TRAVELLING   TURNING   ROLLING
(on hands and feet)   BALANCING   JUMPING

On apparatus
            SWINGING   CLIMBING

To what extent is the child able to:

- practice, improve and refine performance
  - respond imaginatively
  - repeat movements with increasing control and accuracy
- work safely alone, in pairs, in groups
  - plan work with due regard to use of space and safety of others

(ii) Planning

- find solutions to tasks
- select movement content
- design and compose sequences
- share ideas with others

(iii) Evaluating

- make judgements about own and others' performance
  - recognise the movement content and describe compositional features of the sequence
    use appropriate vocabulary to describe the performance
  - appreciate the qualities which make up good performance

(iv) Health-related exercise

- take some responsibility for warming-up and cooling-down activities
- demonstrate safe lifting and carrying technique
- understand the reasons for safe rolling, jumping and landing technique
- talk about the value of exercise in a gymnastic context

As in all Programmes of Study the lessons should begin with body preparation. Activities to raise the heart rate in a gymnastics context should be followed by some stretching and mobilising activities (see Bray, 1993, for practical ideas). There should be a balance between floor and apparatus work. The Gymnastics Activities programme should enable children to develop a variety of skills on the floor and to extend those skills initially by working on low surfaces. Performing on higher platforms, narrower surfaces and swinging and climbing apparatus offer further challenges in solving problems and making decisions in designing and performing sequences. If children are given insufficient time to develop confidence and skilful performance in their floorwork it will be difficult for them to achieve good standards on the apparatus.

A lesson pattern for Gymnastics Activities is suggested:

> *Warm-up* This should include some travelling activities to raise the heart rate and could be related to the theme 'stretching the muscles and mobilising the joints'
> *Floorwork*
> *Apparatus work*
> *Floorwork* (concluding activity).

Dance at Key Stages 1 and 2
The Programmes of Study for Dance are stated:

Key Stage 1
Pupils should be taught (p.3):

(a) to develop control, coordination, balance, poise and elevation in the basic actions of travelling, jumping, turning, gesture and stillness;
(b) to perform movements or patterns, including some from existing dance traditions;
(c) to explore moods and feelings and to develop their response to music through dances, by using rhythmic responses and contrasts of speed, shape, direction and level.

Key Stage 2
Pupils should be taught (p.4):

(a) to compose and control their movements by varying shape, size, direction, level, speed, tension and continuity;
(b) a number of dance forms from different times and places, including some traditional dances of the British Isles;
(c) to express feelings, moods and ideas, to respond to music, and to create simple characters and narratives in response to a range of stimuli, through dance.

A good quality Dance programme will enable children to develop their physical skills, their intellectual abilities, their social and personal skills, it will provide opportunities for them to express and communicate ideas, feelings and emotions through movement. It will also help children to learn about dances in their own and other cultures. Smith-Autard (1995, pages 3 to 6) suggested four ways in which dance is distinctive:

> *dance* provides opportunity for artistic and aesthetic education
> *dance* provides experiences in which children can develop emotionally and learn to express feelings, moods and ideas symbolically, using movement
> *dance* develops rhythmic and musical sensitivity

Key Stage 1 Dance, Reception Year 1, Dancing for joy

dance develops cultural/historical knowledge and understanding of
- the art form
- traditional dance forms of diverse cultures.

Of course, these aspects will only be achieved if teachers have a sound knowledge-base and understand the processes involved to plan a suitable programme for their class. As in other areas of the curriculum there is no one way to teach dance and the teaching styles will vary according to the learning outcomes of the lessons and the needs of the children.

Teachers often cite the difficulty of finding suitable music for dance as a reason for not teaching it. Sometimes it only needs a coordinated approach to realise that within the school there are already many resources available which could be shared.

> **Activity**
> As a group, talk about the music you have used as accompaniment for dance. Share ideas and make a list under themes (festivals, stories, seasons, sporting events, elements, action dances, traditional dances). Talk about how the music was used and which parts were suitable for particular dance ideas.

The coordinator could catalogue the resources, with notes to remind teachers how the music might be used, and make them accessible to all staff. It is also helpful if percussion instruments are stored close to the hall so that they are to hand for teaching dance. Other resources such as poems, stories, pictures, objects and props could also be located at a central point to be used by all the staff.

There are a number of commercial videos available for teachers to enable children to develop a knowledge of dance. These are very valuable as a resource. Many children have not had the opportunity to see a variety of dance performance and because of this have a rather limited view of what might be expected of them in dance lessons. Videos can be used to show children different dance forms and styles or used as a stimulus for them to compose their own dances. Some which have been found to be useful for teaching at Key Stages 1 and 2 are listed in Chapter 5. These could also be stored at a central place and made available to all staff.

Dance is an area of the curriculum which links particularly well to topic work – DES (1991c) reported that some of the best work in dance was seen when cross-curricular links were developed. Work being developed in other areas of the curriculum (for example, Music, Art, Language and Humanities, see Bray and Horton, 1992 and 1994) can provide a rich source of ideas for dance. Similarly dance lessons can be the starting point for other work in the curriculum.

All children must be given equal access to a stimulating dance programme. 'Dance is not primarily a girls' activity, and should not be promoted as such. It is important to ensure that, as teachers we are not giving subliminal messages about dance in the curriculum....Dance is a physical and artistic medium, it requires both strength and sensitivity – attributes which both boys and girls will benefit from acquiring' (Devon County Council, 1996b, p.8).

All children are able to achieve in dance. Children who experience a good quality Dance programme will have opportunities to compose, perform and view dances and learn to describe what they see. They will be able to perform with confidence and have a good understanding of the health benefits through active participation. Most of all a central aim of the Dance programme should be that children enjoy the experiences and value dance as an art form throughout their lives.

As the DES (1991a) pointed out, 'Dance in schools has evolved over the last twenty years from free, expressive movement to more structured experiences' (p.13). The challenge for many teachers is to know how to develop ideas in Dance and plan a structured series of lessons to enable children to develop work of high quality. It is worth stressing that Dance is no more difficult to teach than any other areas of the curriculum and there is no need for teachers to feel that they have to be dancers any more than they need to be athletes to teach Athletics Activities. A sound structure from which to plan, a keen eye to observe the children's responses to tasks and an enthusiasm will go a long way towards developing high standards of achievement.

Since the advent of the National Curriculum there have been several publications which have been written to support the non-specialist teacher in the teaching of Dance (see Chapter 5). However, some of the most exciting work is developed when it is planned in relation to children's own experiences and interests. Therefore it might be helpful to outline some of the structures and processes involved in teaching Dance.

Activity
Curriculum coordinators supporting colleagues might use this framework to work through an idea together as an INSET activity.
 (i) Select the stimulus for dance (for example, music, stories, poems, objects, sculptures, the topic theme, a movement idea). The more children are able to relate to the idea the more imaginative their responses are likely to be.
(ii) Identify the intention of the dance lessons (that is, the

learning outcome) – this will relate to the Programme of Study for Dance and End of Key Stage Descriptions.
(iii) Present the stimulus to the children and ask them for their ideas for movement content and framework. Write their ideas on a board or bright card so that they are all aware of their contributions in the brainstorming session. All dances involve action: during the brainstorming session it will be necessary to identify the body actions which might be appropriate to explore for the dance.

A reminder of the basic actions in dance might be helpful here:

Travelling – on feet or other body parts (stepping, skipping, running, sliding)

Jumping – there are five basic jumps when the different ways to take off and land are taken into account, ie one foot to the same foot (hopping), one foot to the other foot (leaping), one foot to two feet, two feet to two feet, two feet to the other foot. Children can also vary the shape of the body in flight and the expressive quality of the jumping action (a jump for joy will have a different expressive quality and body shape from a jumping action performed to symbolise anger)

Turning – full or part turns using different body parts to lead the way, ie spiralling, whirling, rolling

Gesture – these actions colour the dance and enable intentions to be communicated (hand gestures to greet another person, waving, kicking, facial expressions)

Stillness – can be very effective in dance, eg balancing, pausing, settling.

(iv) Choose the most appropriate ideas and use them to plan the series of lessons. Given that most dance lessons are one hour long at the most, and generally shorter than that, most dance ideas will need to be developed over several lessons to give children adequate time to achieve good standards. Children will need plenty of time to talk about their ideas, try them out, show each other, describe what they and others have done and select the best solutions to the tasks.

Having identified the actions, ie the actions which are going to be developed, the dynamic and spatial aspects need to be considered. Figure 4.2 is offered as guidance for planning.

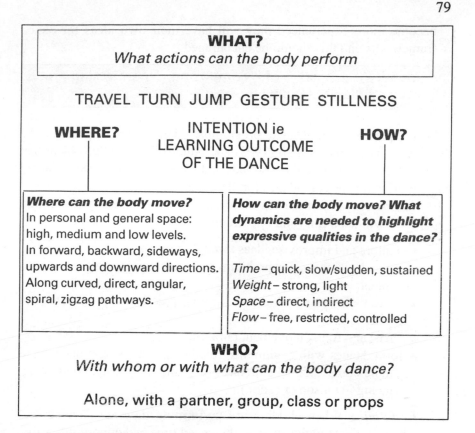

WHAT?
What actions can the body perform

TRAVEL TURN JUMP GESTURE STILLNESS

WHERE?

INTENTION ie
LEARNING OUTCOME
OF THE DANCE

HOW?

Where can the body move?
In personal and general space:
high, medium and low levels.
In forward, backward, sideways,
upwards and downward directions.
Along curved, direct, angular,
spiral, zigzag pathways.

*How can the body move? What
dynamics are needed to highlight
expressive qualities in the dance?*

Time – quick, slow/sudden, sustained
Weight – strong, light
Space – direct, indirect
Flow – free, restricted, controlled

WHO?
With whom or with what can the body dance?

Alone, with a partner, group, class or props

Figure 4.2 Guidance for planning

However simple the dances may be they should have clear beginnings, middles and ends. The form of the finished dance may be created by use of variation, contrast, repetition, unity, transitions and highlights. The structure or sequential form of dance often relates to form in music and the same terms may be used:

Binary form AB: the dance is in two parts
Tertiary form ABA: the beginning of the dance is repeated at the end
Rondo form ABACA: as in a song the dance is like verse and chorus
Narrative ABCDEF: the dance informs as a story.

Harlow and Rolfe (1992) provided a very comprehensive text for those teachers who have little knowledge and confidence to teach dance. In addition to clearly explaining the principles and processes involved in teaching dance they offered many exciting dance ideas and frameworks. Teachers initially need to provide the framework within which children can create their own dances. As children become more experienced they will have their own ideas for dance frameworks and this should be encouraged.

(v) Identify aspects of composing, performing and appreciating to be developed.

When planning the Dance programme identify the aspects to be developed. The Arts Council (1993) and Autard-Smith (1995) identified components within these three strands and the models have been adapted and are offered here as guidance for planning:

Composing This involves children in making their own dances. They will need time and opportunities to:

- explore and improvise ideas through movement;
- make decisions, solve problems and select appropriate movement content;
- share their ideas with others through practical demonstration or discussion;
- shape and refine movement phrases;
- form dances with beginnings, middles and ends, and understand simple compositional structures (copying, mirroring, contrasting, dancing in unison or canon).

Performing When children are performing they are dancing and whatever the stimulus or style they need time and opportunities to:

- develop physical skill and a repertoire of actions to travel, turn, jump and perform gestures, to perform a set dance, to express an idea, tell a story or communicate a mood;
- develop the ability to link actions together with control and with smooth transitions;
- repeat simple patterns (eg folk dances);
- perform with clarity of body shape in stillness and in action;
- use the appropriate expressive qualities to interpret the idea (eg strong/light, fast/slow);
- move rhythmically;
- develop the ability to use space alone and with others, being aware of different directions, floor and aerial pathways, and high, medium and low levels in personal space;
- be able to cooperate and dance with others in pairs, small groups and whole class activities.

PROGRESSION THROUGH A DANCE PROGRAMME
KEY STAGES 1 AND 2

Reception

- Improvise and explore a variety of actions in response to a range of stimuli (percussion, taped music, nursery rhymes, stories, poems, objects – balloons, springs, mobiles, bubbles, pictures)
- Focus on safe use of space
- Body awareness
- Listening and responding

Throughout the Dance programme there should be opportunities for children to be involved in creating, performing and appreciating

Year 1

Children should be given opportunities to:

Plan (compose)

- listen and respond to guidance from the teacher
- explore and select responses to a variety of stimuli (music, nursery rhymes, stories, poems, pictures, moveable objects)

Perform

- improvise and explore a range of travelling, jumping, turning actions
- use a variety of gestures to express moods, feelings and emotions

Evaluate (appreciate)

- recognise and talk about the content of own and others' dances
- with guidance from the teacher recognise and describe good quality of performance (for example, light/strong movement, clarity of body shape, appropriate response to task)

Year 2

Plan (compose)

- explore, select and refine responses to a variety of stimuli
- create clear starting and finishing positions for simple dances
- plan a series of movements (motif) in response to the task

Perform

- improvise and explore a range of travelling, jumping, turning actions, using a variety of gestures to express moods, feelings and emotions

- link basic actions together with a focus on changes of speed, direction or level
- work alone and with a partner

Evaluate (appreciate)

- describe the movement content of their own or others' work
- with guidance from the teacher comment on the quality of their own and others' performance

Years 3 and 4

Plan (compose)

- improvise and explore a variety of movements and build on the repertoire developed during earlier lessons to focus on increased demands of spatial, qualitative and social elements of their performance

Perform

- a wider range of movements with increased variety in the shape, size, level and complexity of the movement patterns
- simple dances with clear beginnings, middles and ends
- a number of dance forms from different times and places

Evaluate (appreciate)

- describe the movement content of their own and others' work with increased sensitivity
- begin to recognise the structure in the dances

Years 5 and 6

Plan (compose)

- individual, pair and group dances through exploring, selecting, repeating and refining movements, using own and teacher's ideas
- structure dances, making decisions about form and content

Perform

- an increased range of actions with control, coordination, improved balance and poise
- with clarity of body shape in stillness and in action
- with smooth transitions
- expressively and rhythmically
- experience range of dance forms from different times and places

Evaluate (appreciate)

- talk about the dances performed by themselves and others
- identify the actions, qualitative and spatial features of the dances
- recognise the meaning of the dances
- comprehend the structure and form of the dances

Appreciating Children should be given the time and opportunity to view dances. This may be achieved in several ways (in class by performing to each other, recording their own work or the work of others on video or viewing the work of professional artists). Children should be given the time and opportunity to:

- learn to watch carefully and to identify features of performance which have been highlighted by the teacher (the movement content, expressive qualities or compositional features);
- develop a vocabulary with which to describe what they see;

- recognise difference in style and form;
- identify the differences in dances which they experience from different times and different cultures;
- evaluate their own and others' performance.

In addition, curriculum coordinators planning the Dance curriculum across Key Stages 1 and 2 might find the following representation of progression through the programme a useful source for reference.

If facilities and timetabling do not enable children to experience dance lessons every week, development and progression will be best achieved if children have blocks of work .

A lesson pattern for Dance is suggested:

- Warm-up this should include some travelling activities to raise the heart rate and could be related to the theme 'stretching the muscles and mobilising the joints'
- Introduction or development of the stimulus
- Selecting and refining the content of the dances
- Performing and viewing the dances
- Concluding activity.

ASSESSMENT - DANCE   KEY STAGE 1

Consider

(i)   Performing
(ii) Planning (composing)
(iii) Evaluating (appreciating)
(iv) Health-related exercise

(i) Performing

Identify the basic actions the child is able to perform

TRAVELLING	JUMPING	TURNING
GESTURE	STILLNESS	

To what extent is the child able to:

- perform simple skills
  - consider contrasts of speed, shape, direction and level
  - body control, coordination, balance, poise, elevation and resilience in landing

- ability to move rhythmically and expressively
- clarity of body shape in stillness and in action
- show control in linking actions together
  - perform movements or patterns with fluency and control
  - refine and repeat simple dances
- work safely
  - consider the child's ability to change direction and be aware of others
  - in pairs
  - in groups

(ii) Planning (composing)

- plan simple skills
  - improvise, explore and select content for dances
  - compose simple dances with clear beginnings, middles and ends

(iii) Evaluating (appreciating)

- with guidance on what to look for, describe the content and some of the expressive qualities of their own and others' dances

(iv) Health-related exercise

- recognise and describe the changes that happen to the body during exercise
  - in warm-up activities to raise the heart rate, stretch the muscles and mobilise the joints

---

ASSESSMENT - DANCE   KEY STAGE 2

Consider

   (i)   Performing
   (ii) Planning (composing)
   (iii) Evaluating (appreciating)
   (iv) Health-related exercise

(i) Performing

Identify the basic actions the child is able to perform

| TRAVELLING | JUMPING | TURNING |
| GESTURE | | STILLNESS |

To what extent is the child able to:

- practice, improve and refine performance
  - control the movements by varying shape, size, direction, level, speed and continuity
  - shape and refine movement phases
  - move rhythmically and expressively
  - link actions together with fluency and smooth transitions
- repeat series of movement
  - repeat simple patterns
- work safely alone, in pairs and in groups
  - use space with an awareness of others
  - perform actions with technical competence with regard to personal safety

(ii) Planning (composing)

- find solutions, sometimes responding imaginatively
  - explore and improvise
  - select movements to express feelings, moods and ideas
  - create simple characters and narratives
  - structure simple dances
  - respond to music

(iii) Evaluating (appreciating)

- make simple judgements about their own and others' performance
  - observe critically and describe performance using appropriate vocabulary
  - recognise differences in style and form
  - identify the differences in dances from different times and different cultures

(iv) Health-related exercise

- take some responsibility for warming-up and cooling-down activities
- talk about the contribution of dance activity to health and fitness

CHAPTER 5

Resources for Teaching Physical Education

Partnerships in provision

It is recognised that the range of opportunities for children to participate in physical activity in the wider community has increased in recent years (DES/WO, 1991a, 1991b). There has also been an increase in the number of agencies offering schools support in the teaching of sport and dance. It is vital that schools recognise that they play a key role in the provision of the Physical Education curriculum and that cooperation with others will enhance children's experiences and not replace a well planned Physical Education programme. Teachers need to keep in mind that it is they who understand the physical, intellectual, emotional and social needs of their particular class and that although other providers may well be knowledgeable in their activity areas, it is the teacher who knows the child. Teachers, however, welcome support and the popularity of schemes on offer reflect this interest.

Human resources

Many of the national governing bodies of sport have youth development officers who work in partnership with the community to promote and develop their specific sport. Some of the officers have a brief to work with schools either by organising courses for teachers at a central location after school or by visiting schools on a regular basis to introduce the sport and to help teachers work with their classes. The specific sport national governing headquarters will be able to advise on provision in your area. (Some useful addresses are to be found at the end of this chapter.)

Dance companies

Most dance companies have education departments and an officer who has responsibility for coordinating work with schools and will arrange dance residencies. This may involve some of the dancers working in school when the company are performing locally. This enables teachers and children to experience dance workshops usually related to the company's current production, and often followed up with an opportunity for the children to attend the performance and meet the company and so gain a better understanding of the professional work, and dance in general. Artistes who are able to offer a variety of expertise often welcome the opportunity to work in schools (local arts centres will provide details).

Outdoor and Adventurous Activities

Outdoor and Adventurous Activities must be taught at some stage during Key Stage 2. The requirements of the Order could take place entirely in the school environment as nowhere is it stated that schools must include activities such as canoeing, rock-climbing or camping. Outdoor challenges of a problem-solving nature and orienteering activities will form the basis of the work. However if schools wish to broaden the programme there are numerous providers to help enhance the curriculum. The support will range from personnel visiting the school, to children visiting activity or residential centres on a daily or weekly basis. Whatever the situation, 'In all cases, schools must be fully aware of and adhere to school, LEA, DFEE and national governing body requirements for these types of activities' (Martin et al., 1995).

Facilities

Facilities in Primary schools vary throughout the country. Some schools are well provided for with purpose built gymnasia, special halls for dance and drama, and large playgrounds and fields. Others have to make do with less adequate provision. OFSTED (1995a) reported a variety of standards in the quality of accommodation and also found that some outdoor accommodation was inadequately maintained and unsafe. Schools have a responsibility for the safety of their pupils and may need to address the state of repair of the facilities to provide a safe environment. Implementing the Order for Physical Education is without doubt made more difficult for schools who have no school hall, although enthusiastic teachers have made good use of classroom space in teaching floorwork in Gymnastic Activities and Dance. However, DES (1991c) have reported that when indoor space was limited most of the work in small rural Primary schools was taught outside. Schools with limited outdoor space will find more difficulty in teaching games and athletics activities and might need to approach another school or the local community to use their facilities to deliver those Programmes of Study. To make maximum use of the available space playground and field markings will aid organisation. Many schools already have netball court markings on the playground and a line drawn down the middle will give 6 grids to help teachers organise a class for group work (see Figure 5.1). Circles, goals, stopping and starting lines will all help to make managing order easier for the teacher. More imaginative markings could be used for warm-up games, problem-solving activities and a basis from which children can create their own games.

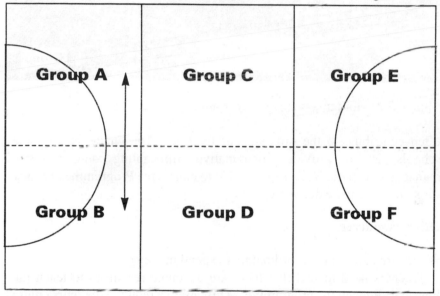

Figure 5.1 A Suggestion for Organisation of Small Group Games on a Netball Court

The requirement in the National Curriculum for all children to learn to swim by the end of Key Stage 2 will have resource implications for all schools. The provision of facilities for swimming ranges from on-site learner pools to community pools which require pupils to travel. The report of the DES survey (1991b) found that a quarter of the schools surveyed had on-site facilities or shared a pool with a local school. Many LEAs have a policy that all Primary pupils should receive swimming tuition and continue to provide some funds to schools even since the introduction of local management of schools. Governors and parents have always recognised the value of swimming in the curriculum and

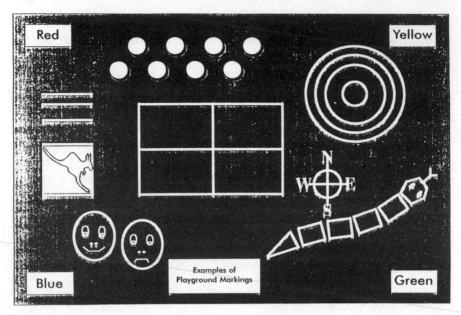

Figure 5.2 More imaginative playground markings

often contribute to the provision of facilities. The challenge to some schools is to provide 'imaginative timetabling and resource management' (DES/WO, 1991b, p.13) to enable the Programme of Study for swimming to be delivered.

Other resources

Where are curriculum coordinators to spend money?

Teachers need to feel that there are adequate resources to teach the Physical Education programme. This might require the curriculum coordinator to draw the whole staff together to discuss provision. It is sometimes the case that resources are available and staff simply do not know of their existence or had not realised the potential use. However, new resources may need to be bought to inspire a fresh teaching approach or to develop a new programme of activity. There have been many new materials produced in the last few years to help the non-specialist teacher to plan for progression in Physical Education. Some of these are described here to help coordinators select support materials in consultation with colleagues.

Athletics Activities

Athletics Activities must be taught at some stage during Key Stage 2 and the following materials will be useful in supporting teachers in their planning and teaching.

Book

The Development of Games and Athletics Skills. Cooper, A. (1993). Hemel Hempstead: Simon and Schuster.

> In addition to the comprehensive coverage of Games, this book provides a scheme of work for Athletics Activities for each year in Key Stage 2. It is written in the light of National Curriculum requirements and gives sound advice on safe management and organisation of groups and equipment. All the practical activities are clearly explained and supported with diagrams. It is the most comprehensive text for Primary schools for delivering programmes for Games and Athletics Activities at Key Stage 2.

Other materials

Athletics. Devon County Council (1996). Torquay: Devon Learning Resources.

> The best resource for practical advice to help children to set themselves realistic and personal challenges. The strength of the materials lies in the way that each activity is presented. Each activity is diagramatically represented and provides sufficient information for children to set up their own activities.

Athletics at Key Stage 2. In *Teaching Physical Education at Key Stages 1 and 2.* Fry, B. (1995). London: P.E.A.

> These materials give advice on planning for progression and an example of medium term planning to plan a unit of work. Safety and developing technical competence in Athletics Activities feature in the publication. Practical activities for eight running tasks, six jumping tasks and six throwing tasks are well presented, stating the purpose, equipment, organisation, procedure and ideas for variations.

There are several commercial schemes to support the teaching of Athletics Activities:

IBM Ten Step Award
Five Star Award Scheme
Milk in Action.

Any coordinators considering organising a sports day will find articles in *Primary Focus* very helpful for ideas for alternative activities.

Dance

Books

Inspirations for Dance and Movement. Evans, J. and Powell, H. (1994). Leamington Spa: Scholastic Publications.

This book is particularly helpful in that it provides stimulating ideas for cross-curricular links. It offers a practical interpretation of the content and language of Dance and presents lesson ideas in an accessible way using a topic-based approach and a model for assessment. Learning outcomes are highlighted and the ideas for both Key Stages 1 and 2 are presented in relation to composing, performing and appreciating. The follow-up ideas will be welcomed by many teachers.

Look! Look what I can do! Creative action ideas for under sevens. Harrison, K. (1990). London: BBC.

A book which succeeds in its aims to provide practical advice and many movement ideas which can be adapted for young children of different abilities and maturity. The photographs of children in action are delightful.

Let's Dance. Harlow, M. and Rolfe, L. (1992). London: BBC.

Described in the text, this book contains everything a teacher needs to plan and deliver lively and clearly constructed dance lessons within the framework of the National Curriculum.

Dance at Key Stages 1 and 2. In *Teaching Physical Education at Key Stages 1 and 2.* Smith-Autard, J. (1995). London: P.E.A.

The processes of teaching and learning in Dance are coherently described, all aspects are considered to help teachers make sense of the Order and provide rich experiences for children in dance education. Sample units of work and outlines for planning are presented separately for Key Stages 1 and 2. There is a wealth of practical advice on short, medium and long term planning. The material covers:

Dance in the National Curriculum
Programmes of Study for Dance
Planning for Dance.

The Dance Pack – Dancing across the Primary Curriculum. Devon

County Council (1996). Torquay: Devon Learning Resources.
Just what teachers are always looking for! The booklet offers dance lessons and the tape has accompanying music to support the text.

Videos

The following videos are useful for supporting dance lessons in Primary schools.

Tales of Beatrice Potter
L'Enfant de les Sortièges (see Harlow and Rolfe, 1992), Nederlands Dans Theatre, Virgin Vision Limited VVD382.

Singing in the Rain (see Smith-Autard, 1994) MGM/UA Home Video PES50185.

Sparatus The Bolshoi Ballet, Castle Vision, CV1 2042 (see Bray and Horton, 1994).

The Video Place has a large library of Dance videos and sells videos of productions of professional works.

Games

A new initiative targeted at schools as part of the Sports Council's National Junior Sports Programme is the TOP Programme. Of particular interest for primary schools are the *TOP Play* and *BT TOP Sport* packages. The packages consist of resource cards and equipment. The cards are designed to be used by teachers and children. The activities have been planned to complement the National Curriculum Games Programmes of Study but not to substitute it. Advice is offered to teachers on progression, safety and follow-up games. *TOP Play* is designed for 4 to 9 year olds and focuses on the core games skills of sending, receiving, travelling with a ball, striking and running and jumping. *BT TOP Sport* is designed for 7 to 11 year olds and is more sport specific and progresses towards mini-games of basketball, cricket, hockey, netball, rugby, table tennis and tennis. There is no cost to schools taking part in the scheme.

Since April 1996 58 LEAs have been working in partnership with the Youth Sport Trust, the Sports Council and other agencies to support schools. As the partnership develops there will be opportunities for other schools to take part and curriculum coordinators should contact the Physical Education adviser to find out if their Authority intends taking part in the scheme.

Books

The Development of Games and Athletics Skills. Cooper, A. (1993). Hemel Hempstead: Simon and Schuster. (Described on page 91.)
  The best resource for developing a Games programme.

Games at Key Stages 1 and 2. In *Teaching Physical Education at Key Stages 1 and 2.* Spackman, L., Collin, W. and Kibble, S. (1995). London: P.E.A.
  Games units highlighting learning outcomes, learning activities and focal points for development are provided for Reception through to Year 6. Lesson plans giving ideas for lesson objectives, introductory activities, development and concluding activities are outlined, with suggestions for extension activities.

Gymnastics

Materials

Primary Gymnastics. Coventry LEA (1994).
  A comprehensive resource document which gives advice on creating a safe environment, planning, examples of units of work and lots of examples of gymnastics sessions for both Key Stages 1 and 2. Useful features include photocopiable sheets to help teachers plan apparatus layouts and guidance on assessment, recording and reporting.

A Devon Approach to Physical Education. Curriculum Gymnastics. Devon County Council (1996). Torquay: Devon Learning Resources.
  These materials cover Key Stages 1, 2 and 3. The work is planned around core skills which are developed through a focus. In support of this approach video materials are also available.

Agile. Nelson (1991).
  A set of resource materials for teaching gymnastics to children 8 to 14.

Outdoor and Adventurous Activities

Outdoor and Adventurous Activities. In *Teaching Physical Education at Key Stages 1 and 2.* Martin, B., Bancroft, G., Hore, M. and Roberts, G. (1995). London: P.E.A.
  These are practical curriculum materials for Outdoor and Adventurous Activities which could be organised on the school site. The nature of Outdoor and Adventurous Activities in the primary curriculum, principles of planning and safety are described. Teachers will find the units of work and ideas for resources very accessible. Practical ideas

for orienteering and outdoor challenges are well supported with diagrams to aid organisation.

Swimming

Swimming Teaching and Coaching: Level 1. Cross, R. (1991). Loughborough: Amateur Swimming Association (ASA).
This book addresses the teaching of swimming and the management and organisation of groups. The individual strokes are illustrated with advice on how to correct faults and improve performance.

A Devon Approach to Physical Education – Swimming and Survival. Devon County Council (1996). Torquay: Devon Learning Resources.
A comprehensive document which focuses on developing effective approaches of teaching and learning swimming. Guidance is provided to help teach water confidence. In the section devoted to teaching, specific stroke development key teaching points are highlighted and supported with clear diagrams. There is reference to synchronized swimming, survival and life-saving skills and there is a progressive series of swimming challenges.

Swimming at Key Stage 2. In *Teaching Physical Education at Key Stages 1 and 2*. Elkington, H. and Harrison, J. (1995). London: P.E.A.
Written by leading experts in the world of swimming, these materials offer a rationale for Swimming, give sound advice on the use of resources, and practical advice on safety and organisation. The lesson ideas are presented by task, and guidance is offered to help children fulfil the task and recognise achievement.

Swimming Games and Activities. Gregeen, A. and Noble, J. (1988). London: A & C Black.
The book is full of ideas for helping children to develop confidence in the water and to enjoy playing a variety of games.

Resources available from the Amateur Swimming Association

Swimming Strokes
Learning to Swim
National Curriculum Resource Pack

General

Practical Guides: Physical Education – Teaching within the National Curriculum. Wetton, P. (1992). Leamington Spa: Scholastic Publications.

For those looking for a book to cover all the areas of activity. Cross-curricular links are highlighted throughout and issues such as safety, special needs and assessment are addressed.

Active Games for Children with Movement Problems. Brown, A. (1987). London: Paul Chapman Publishing.
Practical ideas to enable all children to be successful in participating in Games activities.

These are just some of the resources which schools could consider buying. Curriculum coordinators might set up a resource library to keep colleagues informed of current issues and resources. The Physical Education Association of the United Kingdom is the lead body and a central source of information for courses and resources. In addition to the *British Journal of Physical Education*, the PEA publishes the *Primary Focus* which keeps up to date with new resources and offers readers practical ideas for teaching. It also has a bookshop specialising in books on Physical Education, Sport and Dance. Details about subscriptions are available from the PEA.

Useful Addresses

Dance/Gymnastics/Swimming
Amateur Gymnastics Association, Ford Hall, Lilleshall NSC, Newport, Shropshire TF10 9NB (01952 677137).
Amateur Swimming Association, Harold Fern House, Derby Square, Loughborough, Leicestershire LE11 OAL (01509 230431).
Dance Books, 9 Cecil Court, London WC2N 4EZ.
National Dance Teachers Association, 29 Larkspur Avenue, Chasetown, Walsall, Staffordshire WS7 8SR.
National Resource Centre for Dance, University of Surrey, Guildford, Surrey GU2 5XH.
Physical Education Association of the United Kingdom, Suite 5–10 Churchill Square, King's Hill, West Malling, Kent ME19 4DU (01732 875888).
Royal Lifesaving Society UK, Mountbatten House, Studley, Warwickshire B80 7NN (01527 853943).
The Video Place, The Place Theatre, 17 Duke Street, London.
Five Star Award Scheme, Westways,Upper Tadmarton, Nr Banbury, Oxon OX15 5TB.
IBM Ten Step Award, 141–143 Drury Lane, London WC2B STD.
Milk in Action, Education Department, National Dairy Council, 5–7 John Princes Street, London W1M OAP.

Badminton
The English Schools Badminton Association, National Badminton Centre, Bradwell Road, Loughton Lodge, Milton Keynes MK8 9LA (01908 568822).
Mini-Basketball
English Mini-Basketball Association, 44 Northleat Avenue, Paignton, Devon TQ3 3UG (01803 842289).

Cricket
National Cricket Association, Lord's Ground, London NW8 8QZ (0171 289 6098).
Football
The Football Association, 9 Wyllyotts Place, Potters Bar, Hertfordshire EN6 2JH (01707 50057).
Hockey
The Hockey Association, 6 St John's, Worcester WR2 5AH (01905 426009).
Pop Lacrosse
All England Women's Lacrosse Association, 4 Western Court, Bromley Street, Digbeth, Birmingham B9 4AN (0121 773 4422).
Netball
All England Netball Association, 9 Paynes Park, Hitchin, Hertfordshire SG5 1EH (01462 442344).
Rounders
National Rounders Association, 3 Denehurst Avenue, Nottingham NG8 5DA (01602 785514).
Rugby
Rugby Football Union, Resource Centre, Nortonthorpe Mills, Scissett, Huddersfield HD8 9LA (01484 865950).
Tennis
The LTA Trust, The Queen's Club, West Kensington, London W14 9FG (0171 385 4233).
Volleyball
The English Volleyball Association, 27 South Road, West Bridgford, Nottingham NG2 7AG (01602 816324).

Firms supplying Physical Education equipment

Note Before ordering equipment curriculum coordinators would be advised to check with the local authority as many have formed a consortium from which goods may be purchased at competitive rates.

Continental Sports Products Company, Paddock, Huddersfield HDI ASD (01484 539148).
Davies, Ludlow Hill Road, West Brigford, Nottingham NG2 6HD (01602 452203).

References

Agile. Nelson, 1991.

Alexander, R.J. (1992) *Policy and Practice in Primary Education.* London: Routledge.

Allied Dunbar National Fitness Survey (1992) A Report on Activity Patterns and Fitness Levels. London: Sports Council and Health Education Authority.

Almond, L. (1986) 'Reflecting on Themes: A Games Classification', in Thorpe, R.D. (ed.) *Rethinking Games Teaching.* Loughborough: Loughborough University. (pp.71–2)

Almond, L. (ed.) (1989) *The Place of Physical Education in Schools.* London: Kogan Page.

Armstrong, N. and Bray, S. (1991) 'Physical Activity Patterns determined by continuous heart rate monitoring', *Archives of Disease in Childhood,* **66,** 245–7.

Arts Council (1993) *Dance in Schools.* London: Arts Council.

Birmingham City Council (1993) *Safe Use of Gymnastic Apparatus.* Birmingham: National Primary Centre.

Board of Education (1933) *The Syllabus for Physical Training for Schools.* London: HMSO.

Bray, S. (1993) *Fitness Fun. Promoting Health in the Physical Education Programme.* Crediton: Southgate.

Bray, S. and Horton, A (1992) 'Teaching Geography through Dance', *British Journal of Physical Education: Primary Focus,* **23,** 3, 4–5.

Bray, S. and Horton, A. (1994) 'Take an Artefact: Make a Dance', *British Journal of Physical Education: Primary Focus,* **24,** 4, 10–11.

British Advisers and Lecturers in Physical Education (BAALPE) (1995) *Safe Practice in Physical Education.* BAALPE Publication.

British Heart Foundation (1995) *At the heart of education. Exercise and Heart Health.* London: British Heart Foundation.

Brown, A. (1987) *Active Games for Children with Movement Problems.* London: Paul Chapman Publishing.

Carney, C. (1994) Physical Education in Primary Initial Teacher Training in

England and Wales. Paper presented to Physical Education Association of the United Kingdom, Higher Education Interest Group, Standing Conference on Physical Education, Bedford.

Carroll, B. (1995) *Assessment in Physical Education: A Teacher's Guide to Issues*. London: Falmer Press.

Carroll, B. and Hollinshead, G. (1993) 'Equal Opportunities: Race and Gender in Physical Education: A Case Study', in Evans, J. (ed.) *Equality, Education and Physical Education*. London: Falmer Press.

Cooper, A. (1993) *The Development of Games and Athletics Skills*. Hemel Hempstead: Simon and Schuster.

Cooper, A. (1995) *Starting Games Skills*. Cheltenham: Stanley Thornes.

Chedzoy, S. (1995) 'Developing a Curriculum Leadership Role at Key Stage 1 – Physical Education', in Davies, J. (ed.) *Developing a Leadership Role within the Key Stage 1 Curriculum*. London: Falmer Press.

Clay, G. (1995) Preparing for Inspection – Primary Physical Education. Paper presented at the Annual Conference of the Physical Education Association of the United Kingdom. London.

Cross, R. (1991) *Swimming Teaching and Coaching: Level 1*. Loughborough: Amateur Swimming Association.

Curriculum Council for Wales (CCW) (1992) *Physical Education in the National Curriculum: Non-Statutory Guidance for Teachers*. Cardiff: CCW.

Day, C., Whitaker, P. and Johnson, D. (1990) *Managing Primary Schools in the 1990s*. London: Paul Chapman Publishing.

Day, C., Hall C., Gammage, P. and Coles, M. (1993) *Leadership and the Curriculum in the Primary School*. London: Paul Chapman Publishing.

Department for Education (DFE) (1995) Circular 14/93 *Criteria for Initial Teacher Training (Primary Phase)*. HMSO: London.

Department for Education (1995a) *Physical Education in the National Curriculum*. London: HMSO.

Department for Education (1995b) *Science in the National Curriculum*. London: HMSO.

Department of Education and Science (DES) (1978) *Primary Schools in England – A Survey by HM Inspectors of Schools*. London: HMSO.

Department of Education and Science/Welsh Office (1991a) National Curriculum Physical Education Working Group Interim Report. London: DES.

Department of Education and Science/Welsh Office (1991b) Physical Education for ages 5 to 16. Proposals of the Secretary of State for Education and Science and the Secretary of State for Wales. London: HMSO.

Department of Education and Science (1991c) *The Teaching and Learning of Physical Education*. London: HMSO.

DES (1992) *Physical Education in the National Curriculum*. London: HMSO.

Department of National Heritage (1995) *Sport – Raising the Game*. London: Department of National Heritage.

Devon Curriculum Advice (1994) *A Devon Approach to Teaching Games*.

102

Torquay: Devon County Council.

Devon County Council (1996) *A Devon Approach to Physical Education. Curriculum Gymnastics*. Torquay: Devon Learning Resources.

Devon County Council (1996) *A Devon Approach to Physical Education. Dance at Key Stages 2, 3 and 4*. Torquay: Devon County Council.

Devon County Council (1996) *A Devon Approach to Physical Education – Swimming and Survival*. Torquay: Devon Learning Resources.

Devon County Council (1996) *Athletics*. Torquay: Devon Learning Resources.

Devon County Council (1996) *The Dance Pack – Dancing across the Primary Curriculum*. Torquay: Devon Learning Resources.

Duigan, P. (1987) 'Leaders as Culture Builders', *Unicorn*, **13**, 4, pp.208–14, cited in Day, C., Hall C., Gammage, P. and Coles, M. (1993) *Leadership and the Curriculum in the Primary School*. London: Paul Chapman Publishing.

Elkington, H. and Harrison, J. (1995) 'Swimming at Key Stage 2', in *Teaching Physical Education at Key Stages 1 and 2*. London: Physical Education Association.

• Evans, J. (1993) *Equality, Education and Physical Education*. London: Falmer Press.

Evans, J. and Powell, H. (1994) *Inspirations for Dance and Movement*. Leamington Spa: Scholastic Publications.

Fry, B. (1995) 'Athletics at Key Stage 2', in *Teaching Physical Education at Key Stages 1 and 2*. London: Physical Education Association.

Jones, C. (1996) 'Physical Education at Key Stage 1', in Armstrong, N. (ed.) *New Directions in Physical Education*. London: Cassell.

Harlow, M. and Rolfe, L. (1992) *Let's Dance*. London: BBC.

Harris, J. and Elbourn, J. (1990) *Action for Heart Health: A Practical Health-Related Exercise Programme for Physical Education*. Loughborough: University of Loughborough.

Harris, J. and Elbourn J. (1992) *Warming up and cooling down: practical ideas for implementing the Physical Education National Curriculum*. Loughborough: University of Loughborough.

Harrison, K. (1990) *Look! Look what I can do! Creative action ideas for under sevens*. London: BBC.

Harrison, M. and Cross, A. (1994) 'Successful Curriculum Change Through Coordination', in Harrison, M. (ed.) *Beyond the Core Curriculum*. Plymouth: Northcote House.

Harrison, M. and Theaker, K. (1989) *Curriculum Leadership and Coordination in the Primary School*. Whalley: Guild House Press.

Health Education Authority (1990) *Happy Heart*. Walton-on-Thames: Nelson and Sons.

Health Education Authority (1991) *Teachers' Guide, My Body*. London: Heinemann.

Heath, W., Gregory, C., Money, J., Peat, G., Smith, J. and Stratton, G. (1994) *Blueprints Physical Education Key Stage 1*. Cheltenham: Stanley Thornes.

• Heath, W., Smith, J., Gregory, C., Money, J., Stratton, G., Peat, G. and Bishop,

D. (1994) *Blueprints Physical Education Key Stage 2*. Cheltenham: Stanley Thornes.

Holly, P. and Southworth, G. (1989) *The Developing School*. London: Falmer Press.

House of Commons Select Committee (1986) *Achievement in Primary Schools Volume 1*. London: HMSO.

Howard, J. and West, M. (1991) *Management Development Project. The Co-ordinator Role in Schools*. Cambridge: Cambridge Institute of Education.

Martin, B., Bancroft, G., Hore, M. and Roberts, G. (1995) 'Outdoor and Adventurous Activities', in *Teaching Physical Education at Key Stages 1 and 2*. London: Physical Education Association.

Maude, T. (1994) *The Gym Kit*. Cambridge: Homerton College.

Mawer, M. (1995) *The Effective Teaching of Physical Education*. London: Longman.

National Curriculum Council (NCC) (1992) *Physical Education Non-Statutory Guidance*. York: NCC.

Office for Standards in Education (OFSTED) (1995a) *Physical Education – A review of inspection findings 1993/1994*. London: HMSO.

OFSTED (1995b) *Guidance on the Inspection of Nursery and Primary Schools*. London: HMSO.

OFSTED (1995c) *Physical Education and Sport in Schools – A Survey of Good Practice*. London: HMSO.

Physical Education Association of the United Kingdom (PEA) (1995) *Teaching Physical Education at Key Stages 1 and 2*. London: Physical Education Association.

Powell, K.E., Thompson, P.D., Casperson, C.J. and Kendrick, J.S. (1987) Physical Activity and the Incidence of Coronary Heart Disease. *Annual Review of Public Health*, 8, 253-87.

School Curriculum and Assessment Authority (SCAA) (1993) *The National Curriculum and its Assessment*. London: SCAA Publications.

School Curriculum and Assessment Authority (SCAA) (1995) *Planning the Curriculum at Key Stages 1 and 2*. London: SCAA Publications.

Sleap, M. (1995) *Skip for Health*. Hull: University of Hull.

Sleap, M. and Warburton, P. (1992) 'Physical Activity Levels of 5–11 year-old children in England as determined by continuous observation', *Research Quarterly for Exercise and Sport*, 63, 238–245.

Smith-Autard, J. (1994) *The Art of Dance*. London: A & C Black.

Smith-Autard, J. (1995) 'Dance at Key Stages 1 and 2', in *Teaching Physical Education at Key Stages 1 and 2*. London: Physical Education Association.

Spackman, L., Collin, W. and Kibble S. (1995) 'Games at Key Stages 1 and 2', in *Teaching Physical Education at Key Stages 1 and 2*. London: Physical Education Association.

Sugden, D. and Wright, H. (1996) 'Curricular Entitlement and Implementation for all Children', in Armstrong, N. (ed.) *New Directions in Physical Education*. London: Cassell. (pp.110–30)

Thorpe, R. (1990) 'New Directions in Games Teaching', in Armstrong, N. (ed.) *New Directions in Physical Education*. Leeds: Human Kinetics.

Thorpe, R.D. and Bunker, D.J. (1989) 'A Changing Focus in Games Education', in Almond, L. (ed.) *The Place of Physical Education in Schools*. London: Kogan Paul. (pp42–71)

Thorpe, R.D., Bunker, D.J. and Almond, L. (1984) 'A Change in Focus for the Teaching of Games', in Pieron, M. and Graham, G. (eds) The 1984 Olympic Scientific Congress Proceedings, Volume 6: Sport Pedagogy. Champaign, Illinois: Human Kinetics.

Wetton, P. (1992) *Practical Guides: Physical Education – Teaching within the National Curriculum*. Leamington Spa: Scholastic Publications.

Williams, A. (1993) 'Who Cares About Girls? Equality, Physical Education and the Primary School Child', in Evans, J. (ed.) *Equality, Education and Physical Education*. London: Falmer Press.

Williams, A. (1996) 'Physical Education at Key Stage 2', in Armstrong, N. (ed.) *New Directions in Physical Education*. London: Cassell.

Williamson, T. (1984) 'Curriculum Leadership in Physical Education: A Case Study Approach to Analysing the Problems, Constraints and Successes. Training the Curriculum Leader.', *The Bulletin of Physical Education*, **20**, 3, pp.16–26.

Williamson, T. (1993) 'Activity – specific Module 3, Games', in Robinson, S. *Physical Education in the Primary School – A school development programme*. Bristol: University of the West of England.

Index